Structure and the
Social Studies

Structure and the
Social Studies

By William T. Lowe

Associate Professor of Education
University of Rochester

Cornell University Press

Ithaca and London

First published 1969

Library of Congress Catalog Card Number: 69-18360

Printed in the United States of America
by The Vail-Ballou Press, Inc.

Preface

This volume had its beginnings in a series of workshops held at Cornell University to study the curriculum revision movement in elementary and secondary school social studies. About fifty teachers of history, geography, and the social sciences from central New York State participated, representing all levels of instruction from kindergarten through graduate school. The workshops were financially supported by two teacher education projects at Cornell, which in turn were assisted by the Ford Foundation, the University, and some twenty school districts in the Ithaca area.

At the heart of the project, and of this book, was the concept of structure. The idea will be analyzed in considerable detail in Chapter 2, but the reader should be aware at the outset that the study began with a tentative position that any discipline worthy of inclusion in the curriculum must have some basic and developmental ideas—both substantive and methodological—to form the core of what is taught in elementary and secondary schools and that the first job of a curriculum builder should be to identify the structural content of the curriculum. The study group believed that the notion of structure has been tremendously important in the curriculum ferment of the sixties.

Preface

A number of distinguished historians and social scientists were invited to apply this partial definition of "structure" to their fields. Chapters 4 through 8 present their response to this challenge.

The first two chapters introduce this presentation. Chapter 1 surveys current activity in social studies curriculum development and describes some of the problems and issues that serve as underpinning for most projects. Chapter 2 analyzes the concept of structure in detail. It argues that although the concept has received little analytic attention, it has influenced nearly all curriculum revision efforts in the area. The third chapter tries to cope with the peculiar and complex problems of applying the idea of structure to the subject of history. It also contains an outline of some content suggestions provided by the three historians who served as consultants and tries to explain why most members of the study group became convinced that structure is not a very useful idea in the development of a curriculum in history.

The format and style of the essays which follow vary sharply. Since we were unwilling to prescribe a pattern for our consultants, who would probably have rejected any such attempt anyway, this variety seems necessary. I have at all times tried to make clear, by the careful use of "we" and "I," which conclusions are those of the study group and which are my own.

I am deeply indebted to the participants in the project, to our consultants, and to several of my students, particularly Miss Harriet Kern, a brilliant teacher of history and now a student of curriculum at Harvard University.

W. T. L.

Rochester, New York
November 1968

Contents

Contents

[viii]

Contents

*Structure and the
Social Studies*

[I]

Social Studies
Curriculum Revision

Climate for Change

In the last few years social studies has belatedly joined the curriculum revolution of the sixties that began in the foreign languages and natural sciences and has now engulfed nearly all traditional subjects. This is a time of ferment in terms of both content and method in the social sciences and history. Very few significant curriculum changes had occurred in the area in the previous forty or fifty years,[1] and most educators agreed that some type of revision was badly needed and long overdue. To be sure, there is no agreement over the specific directions the change ought to take, but that the amount of revision activity has greatly increased is indisputable.

More than fifty projects of national scope were under way in 1968. Federal money was finally flowing, even though not to the same extent as in the "hard sciences." Beginning in 1963, Project Social Studies of the United States Office of Education (U.S.O.E.) instituted a number of curriculum

---

[1] For a succinct historical survey see Erling Hunt and others, *High School Social Studies Perspectives* (Boston: Houghton Mifflin, 1962).

centers in universities. Although the Project itself was dis-
continued in 1966, a number of the centers are quite productive. New national and regional efforts are also being
funded by the U.S.O.E. The National Science Foundation is
sponsoring a major study in anthropology, one in sociology,
and another in geography. Local curriculum efforts under
Titles I and III of the historic Elementary and Secondary
Education Act of 1965 are in progress all over the country,
and many of them are in social studies. Some of the social
studies—history, economics, civics, and geography—are at
last a part of the National Defense Education Act, providing
in-service programs for teachers, more and better instructional materials, and the like. Besides Washington, other
sources of support are now available—foundations, public
school systems, huge new publishing-electronics combines
that have entered the education business, states, regional
groups of schools, professional associations, and others. The
flood is so great that it is difficult for even a devoted professional to keep abreast of developments.[2]

Why has all this activity occurred after so many years of
calm? It is difficult to say, partly because we are still so close
to the events, but at least five factors are probably involved:

1. One cause may be the anxiety phenomenon. Americans are confused and bewildered by foreign relations. We
are afraid of international bogeymen, and the scientific ad-
vances of our "opponents" have forced us to look for a
scapegoat. The schools in general and the social studies
curriculum specifically were readily available for this pur-

[2] *Social Education,* published by the National Council for the Social Studies, is particularly helpful in trying to stay informed. Also
see Edwin Fenton, *The New Social Studies* (New York: Holt, Rinehart and Winston, 1967), and Mark M. Krug, *History and the Social
Sciences* (Waltham, Mass.: Blaisdell, 1967).

pose. Anxieties related to domestic affairs—crime, civil disorder, racial tension—may also have contributed to the revision movement. The social studies program is supposed to help us understand ourselves and live effectively in our society. When great numbers of us are bewildered by our social environment, we are bound to wonder if something might not be wrong with our preparation.

2. The second factor might be called the "bandwagon effect." Foreign languages, mathematics, and science have received money and recognition partly because they were having a curriculum revolution. Linguists, mathematicians, and natural scientists, instead of maintaining their aloofness, began to write curriculum guides and in other ways to associate themselves more closely with public schools. Social studies educators were envious and wanted similar support from social scientists, historians, and geographers.

3. As we have said, money became available. Without involving ourselves in the chicken-versus-egg question, we may safely say that the availability of money has stimulated some of this activity—although, to be sure, the activity has also stimulated the availability of funds.

4. The desire for change for its own sake should be mentioned. Change is in the air. Some people deem an old curriculum a bad curriculum, and the traditional social studies program was old.

5. Finally, and of greatest importance, has been basic dissatisfaction with the status quo. The other four factors might lead the reader to believe that curriculum activity is just a fad or that it would have occurred even if everyone had been happy with the existing program. This is not the case. The existing program was not popular. The serious and substantial criticism that it evoked is at the heart of the current ferment.

[3]

Structure and the Social Studies

What specifically is being criticized by whom? Complaints have been many and various, but before we consider them, it should be understood that they cannot all be valid, at least at the same time, for they are often contradictory. But, accurate or not, the amount of critical comment would in itself be reason to examine seriously what educators are doing.

The students themselves, at least those in the secondary schools, have been very critical. Every popularity poll seems to place the secondary school social studies courses at or near the bottom of the list, with world history as the least popular. Students, particularly bright students, do not elect social studies as one of their fields of concentration unless they are forced to do so. Yet the social studies part of the elementary school program is popular. Something is wrong. Clearly, a study of man ought to be exciting.

And pupils are not the only unhappy ones. The public, both individuals and groups, seem to be more vocally critical than ever before. It would be comforting to believe that censorship or attempts at censorship are on the decline; at least two accounts claim, however, that just the opposite is the case.[3] Critical interest in the schools is a good thing; attempts to use them for the particular whims of particular groups are not. Most of these pressures are directed toward the social studies program. A dissatisfied person finds a like-minded group and the battle is on. Too many of these vigilance groups are highly successful. The point here, however, is that they are active and are a part of the clamor for change, change which could go in many directions.

Vested interest groups and secondary school pupils are

3 Jack Nelson and Gene Roberts, *The Censors and the Schools* (Boston: Little, Brown, 1963), and Mary Anne Raywid, *The Ax-Grinders* (New York: Macmillan, 1962).

[4]

joined by a host of professionals—educationists, historians, social scientists, journalists, and even submariners. Martin Mayer's tirade may still be the best single source from which to get the flavor of these criticisms.[4] Not that these critics are saying the same thing. But they are all emphatically dissatisfied; their voices swell the chorus.

Finally, there is an even more significant group of critics as far as sheer quantity is concerned. Teachers of social studies in elementary and secondary schools are themselves dissatisfied with the status quo. In at least one study on this subject, a sample of social studies teachers were sharply critical of what they were doing and indicated the need for immediate curriculum improvement. In fact, these respondents engaged in a kind of orgy of self-criticism.[5]

In short, then, the amount of dissatisfaction with the pre-1960 curriculum in the social studies by itself demands our attention. But what are the critics unhappy about?

One major concern seems to be the lack of organization. The most obvious example of this failing, and the one cited most often, is in American history. We are told that American history is taught in some form or other again and again and again, that although some repetition is necessary, we have gone much too far. Furthermore, a good many school districts use texts published by the same company for all their American history programs with the result that children are given the same fare three or four times.

Nor is this the only problem. In modern history, for example, there is clearly an overlap between so-called world history and American history, yet these courses are fre-

---

[4] *Where, When and Why: Social Studies in American Schools* (New York: Harper and Row, 1962).

[5] William T. Lowe, "Do Teachers Want Curriculum Change?" *Social Studies,* LV (March 1964), 96–99.

quently taught as if there were absolutely no connection. My own experience in conducting a survey of the social studies program of a public school system is an example. In a meeting of the entire social studies staff, called by the superintendant at my request, one teacher at each grade level described his course and particularly his purposes to the others. The descriptions evoked genuine amazement on the part of the teachers—they had not had any idea of what their colleagues were trying to do.

A second frequently mentioned criticism—true or false— is the claim that the program is far too provincial. The argument goes that we do not spend nearly enough time and emphasis on the so-called developing regions of the world (Africa, most of Asia, and Latin America) and that when these areas are taught, as someone has said, the instruction takes place from the deck of a gunboat, in the context of European and North American imperialism.

Another part of this criticism is the idea that we spend too much time on the local community and the state. We have all chuckled over the cartoon which depicts a group of primary school children avidly discussing the intricacies of space exploration and then shows their dejection when they must return to the classroom to discuss the fireman, the postman, and the policeman. Then too, while a good many states are dropping their requirements for a full year's work on state and local history and geography, a large number continue this practice. New York, for example, a leading state in the revision movement, still recommends that two-thirds of the seventh grade be spent on state and local topics. Parenthetically, when a "high-powered" ad hoc committee employed by the New York State Education Department recommended the reduction of this emphasis, the State Historical Association waged and won an effective pressure campaign. In short, the provincialism charge might be summarized by the frequently heard comment in up-state New York: "Too many cowboys, too many Indians, and too damn many canals."

A third area of criticism is that not enough social science is taught, or, on the other side of the coin, that too much history is. Anthropology, economics, and geography, particularly, and government, sociology, and social psychology, to a lesser degree, claim that they should be taught as separate subjects or, at least, that some of their principles and concepts should be a part of the program. In fact, as we shall see in more detail, some are arguing that anthropology and cultural geography ought to be the organizing disciplines of the program instead of history.

Most of those who want to reduce or eliminate history realize that they are attacking a bastion of considerable strength. Most secondary school teachers, if they have any depth in any discipline, are trained in history. Furthermore, history has always dominated the "social studies" program. In spite of all this, we are now hearing that history is too sophisticated, too abstract, and too impractical for most secondary school youngsters. Finally, we are told that developing a sense of time is very difficult and probably not worth the effort for many children.

Basic questions centering on the purpose, methods of inquiry, and organization of history remain to be resolved in the minds of professional historians. How then, the argument goes, can we expect immature pupils to understand, indeed even study, history? Some of these arguments will be examined in Chapter 3 of this work.[6]

[6] Some of the arguments are summarized in William T. Lowe, "Where Should History Be Taught?" *Clearing House,* XXXIX (Dec. 1964), 210–213.

Another attack has suggested that the traditional subject disciplines are inappropriate as the basis of a secondary school curriculum. This is, of course, not a new position—in fact, it may well be on the wane. Nevertheless, a list of dissatisfactions would be quite incomplete without mentioning it.

At least three groups with quite different goals in mind take this point of view. One group wants the guidance function of the social studies program strengthened and expanded. They speak in terms of the psycho-social needs of children. These needs, they argue, are or should be the determinant of the program. Another group would emphasize skills. They really do not care what content is taught as long as children learn the wide range of social studies skills —reading, writing, using graphics, using libraries, using maps, data-gathering, analyzing documents, problem-solving, speaking, listening, and so on. Some, for example, argue that our only real purpose ought to be to teach critical thinking, although, of course, there is no precise agreement as to the meaning of "critical thinking." Finally, there are some critics who lament the teaching of anything which is not aimed directly at the learning of certain values. There are a good many lists of these values which have been developed by a variety of sources.[7] Probably most of them could be summarized by the term "effective citizenship." This goal involves more than teaching values, but attitudes and appreciations seem to be at the heart of it. The only belief that these groups share is their disenchantment with using the disciplines to organize the curriculum.

Another frequently heard criticism is that we are simply trying to teach too much. The ground-covering phenome-

[7] See *A Guide to Content in the Social Studies,* published by the National Council for the Social Studies in 1958. This publication does not suggest that values are the only appropriate goal.

non is still with us. The pattern for our present program was set at least as early as 1916 and, clearly, a great deal has happened since then. There has been a scholarship revolution in the social sciences and history as well as in the hard sciences. Also, each new discipline making a claim for time in the social studies curriculum has been accommodated at least to a degree. Our courses, according to this argument, have become overloaded with detail. Neither the students nor the teachers seem to know what is important and what is trivial. Charles Keller of the John Hay fellowship program has said that we ought to start our curriculum investigation by an admission that at least one quarter of the content we are now teaching should be omitted.

A final criticism is the point that the social sciences and history have not turned to scholars for direction and help with the curriculum to the degree that other areas have. Part of this problem, however, has been the lack of money and other resources.

These, then, are the major dissatisfactions which seem to be involved in the urge for change. Now let us briefly outline the status quo. What is the program of studies in the social sciences and history that has been under attack?

The Present Program

The social studies program in 1960 was basically the same as the one of 1930 or earlier. It has been the subject of many surveys, which will not be summarized here. One essay which does just this states categorically that "curriculum offerings in the social studies have changed relatively little in the past fifty years." [8]

[8] F. R. Smith, "The Curriculum," *New Challenges in the Social Studies: Implications of Research for Teaching,* ed. B. Massialas and F. R. Smith (Belmont, Cal.: Wadsworth, 1965), p. 53.

Table 1. Public secondary school social studies program in 1963

Course	Schools offering separate courses (%)	Schools offering the course that require it for graduation (%)	Schools offering the course that provide it at the same grade level (%)
American gov't. (senior high)	58	78	84 (12th)
Civics (junior high)	62	74	52 (9th)
Economics	47	Not available	Not available
Guidance (many different names)	18	Not available	Not available
American history (junior high)	75	94	73 (8th)
Problems of democracy	32	63	93 (12th)
American history (senior high)	93	98	64 (11th)
State history & geography	49	Not available	Not available
World geography	54	53	(Wide range, 7th–10th)
World history	85	51	65 (10th)

Source: S. B. Anderson and others, *Social Studies in Secondary Schools: A Survey of Courses and Practices* (Princeton, N.J.: Educational Testing Service, 1964) ; used by permission of the Educational Testing Service.

Table 1 provides a suggestion of what American secondary school pupils study and when they study it. If these data represent an appropriate sample, then better than half the young people in secondary schools study American history and American government twice in grades seven through twelve. A majority of them also take world history, and world geography. Almost half will be able to study in a separate course of a term or more in length state history, geography, and economics. The most common sequence is:

Grade 7. Geography (second half of a two-year sequence) or state history and geography

Grade 8. United States history

Grade 9. Civics, economics, economic geography, and/or guidance (great variety of required courses at this level)

Grade 10. World history (actually European history) or world geography

Grade 11. American history or world history

Grade 12. American government, economics, and/or problems of democracy

Among elementary schools, as Edwin Carr points out, there is a greater variety than among secondary schools. The following "central tendencies," however, are most common.[9]

Grade 1. Life at home and at school; pets; holidays; farm life

Grade 2. Community helpers and workers; transportation; communication

Grade 3. Expanding community; food, clothing, shelter; other communities

Grade 4. Living in other lands; state history; state geography

Grade 5. United States history and geography; Latin America; Canada; Western Hemisphere

Grade 6. Geography of Western Hemisphere; geography of Eastern Hemisphere; Old World backgrounds of American history

Of course, this outline of course titles does not even hint at some highly significant questions. Clearly, we have not taken a position on whether these are the "right" or the "wrong" courses. Nor have we said anything about the

[9] Edwin Carr, *The Social Studies* (New York: Center for Applied Research in Education, 1965).

actual content of the courses. It is posible that the subject matter of the program has changed while the titles have remained the same. One publication of the National Council for the Social Studies makes just such a claim: "In spite of the persistence of the general pattern recommended in 1916, it would be inaccurate to describe the social studies program as static. Within the subject fields major changes have occurred." [10] Frankly, this seems doubtful, but the point will not be debated here. We can safely say that the course titles we are now using were recommended fifty years ago.

Contemporary Projects

The curriculum ferment of the sixties in the social studies has taken a number of directions. It is too soon to make a detailed evaluation of most of the projects that are currently under way. Nearly all the project directors admit that their materials are still quite tentative, and some of the most promising efforts have accomplished only a modest part of their goals. Short summaries of some of the work are already available; *Social Education,* for example, devotes at least part of one issue each year to keeping its readers informed on the progress of these efforts. But it may be useful here to list some of the projects, even though the list is undoubtedly incomplete and will certainly be out-dated by the time it is published. The titles of the projects will give the reader an idea of the range of topics being studied. Furthermore, the list documents some duplication of effort and some omissions. It also denotes some of the most productive individ-

[10] Willis D. Moreland, *Social Studies in the Senior High School: Programs for Grades Ten, Eleven and Twelve* (Washington, D.C.: National Council for the Social Studies, 1965).

uals, institutions, and funding sources that have been involved in the curriculum revision movement in the social studies.

Anthropology

Anthropology Curriculum Study Project (A.C.S.P.)
   Malcolm Collier
   5632 South Kimbark Ave., Chicago, Illinois 60637
   (Anthropology materials for secondary schools)
   Supported in part by the American Anthropological Association and the National Science Foundation

Development of a Sequential Curriculum in Anthropology for Grades One–Seven, or the Anthropology Curriculum Project
   Marion J. Rice and Wilfred Bailey
   Peabody Hall, University of Georgia, Athens, Georgia
   (Instructional materials in anthropology for grades 1–7)
   Supported in part by U.S.O.E.

Inland Valley Elementary School Archeology Project
   Donald Hardy
   University of California, Berkeley, California
   Supported in part by U.S.O.E.

Economics

Development of Economic Curriculum Materials for Secondary Schools
   (This project uses a variety of titles even in its publications: Ohio State Economic Study, Economics Curriculum Project, Economics Curriculum Materials Project)
   Meno Lovenstein
   Ohio University, Athens, Ohio
   (Economics for grade 9)
   Supported in part by U.S.O.E.

Developmental Economic Education Program of the Joint Council on Economic Education
> John E. Maher
> 1212 Avenue of the Americas, New York, New York 10036
> (Development of economics education in twenty-nine school systems)
> J.C.E.E. formed in 1948—many affiliated state and local associations. Wide support among business, labor, agriculture, and the professions.

Economics 12 Project
> John G. Sperling and Suzanne E. Wiggins
> San Jose State College, San Jose, California 95114
> (A grade 12 course in economics for students of all abilities)
> Supported in part by U.S.O.E.

Elementary School Economics Program
> William Rader
> Industrial Relations Center, University of Chicago, Chicago, Illinois 60637
> (Economics materials for grades 4–8)
> Supported in part by the Center

Elkhart, Indiana, Experiment in Economic Education
> Lawrence Senesh
> Purdue University, Lafayette, Indiana 47907
> (The program's published title is *Our Working World*, Science Research Associates)
> Supported by a variety of sources including the Carnegie Foundation

Harvard-Newton Project in Business History and Economic Concepts
> Paul E. Cawein
> Newton Public Schools, Newton, Massachusetts 02159
> (Historical development of businesses for children)
> Supported by at least sixteen different businesses, foundations, and educational institutions

Production and Evaluation of Three Computer-Based Economic Games for Sixth Grade
  Richard L. Wing
  Yorktown Heights, New York
  (Computer-assisted instruction)
  Supported in part by U.S.O.E.

General—Multidisciplinary

Chicago Social Studies Project
  Edgar Bernstein
  University of Chicago, 1362 E. 59th St., Chicago, Illinois
      60637
  (Materials for grades 9–10 social studies, integrating history
      and social science)
  Supported in part by U.S.O.E.

A Conceptual Framework for the Social Studies in Wisconsin
Schools
  Department of Instruction, Madison, Wisconsin
  (Broadly based social studies program)
  Supported by the State

Demonstration to Improve the Teaching of Social Studies—
Grades One–Six
  Merle W. Vance
  Sacramento State College, Sacramento, California
  Supported in part by U.S.O.E.

Development of a Comprehensive Curriculum Model for
Social Studies Grades One-Eight, also Taba Curriculum Development Project
  Norman E. Wallen
  Education Building, San Francisco State College, San Francisco, Calif. 94132
(Comprehensive social studies program for grades 1–8)
  Supported in part by U.S.O.E.

Development of a Model for the St. Louis Metropolitan Social Studies Center
　Harold Berlak and Judson Shaplin
　Washington University, St. Louis, Missouri 63130
　(Grades K–12)
　Supported in part by U. S. O. E.

Greater Cleveland Social Science Program
　Raymond English
　Rockefeller Building, 614 W. Superior Ave., Fourth Floor, Cleveland, Ohio 44113
　(Social studies materials for grades K–12)
　Supported by a variety of sources including the Kettering, Cleveland, and Jennings foundations

Harvard Social Studies Project, also The Analysis of Public Controversy: A Study in Citizenship Education Social Studies Project
　Donald Oliver and Fred Newman
　Roy E. Larsen Hall, Appian Way, Graduate School of Education, Harvard University, Cambridge, Massachusetts 02138
　(Instructional materials, grades 7–10)
　Supported in part by U.S.O.E.

Identification of Major Social Science Concepts and Their Utilization in Instructional Materials
　Roy A. Price
　409 Maxwell Hall, Syracuse University, Syracuse, New York 13210
　(Preparation of materials based on the thirty-four key concepts developed by the project)
　Supported in part by U.S.O.E.

Lincoln Filene Center for Citizenship and Public Affairs
　John S. Gibson
　Tufts University, Medford, Massachusetts 02155

　[16]

Curriculum Revision

(Teaching materials and research on many topics including race and culture in America, dating back to 1948)
Supported by many sources including U.S.O.E.

Preparation and Evaluation of Social Studies Curriculum Guides and Materials for Grades K–Fourteen, or Project Social Studies Curriculum Center
Edith West
College of Education, University of Minnesota, Minneapolis, Minnesota 55455
(Centered around concept of culture, grades K–14)
Supported in part by U.S.O.E.

Report of the State Central Committee on Social Studies to the California State Curriculum Commission
California State Department of Education, Sacramento, California
(Comprehensive program)
Supported by the State

A Secondary School Social Studies Curriculum Focused on Thinking Reflectively about Public Issues
James P. Shaver
Utah State University, Logan, Utah
Supported in part by U.S.O.E.

Sequential Social Studies Program for the Secondary School, or Social Science Curriculum Study Center
Ella C. Leppert
University High School, University of Illinois, Urbana, Illinois 61806
(Multidisciplinary programs, grades 8–10)
Supported in part by U.S.O.E.

Social Science Education Consortium
Irving Morrissett
1424 North 15th St., Boulder, Colorado 80304

(Encouragement and publicizing of innovative practices of
many sorts, grades K–12; very useful newsletter)
Formerly supported by U.S.O.E.

Social Studies Curriculum Center: A Sequential Curriculum on
American Society for Grades 5–12
John R. Lee
Northwestern University, Evanston, Illinois 60201
(Public domain materials available)
Supported in part by U.S.O.E.

Social Studies Curriculum Program
Peter Dow
Educational Development Center (formerly Educational Ser-
vices Incorporated), 15 Mifflin Place, Cambridge, Massa-
chusetts 02138
(Complete program, grades K–12)
Supported by many sources including U.S.O.E.

Social Studies Curriculum Project
Edwin Fenton
Carnegie-Mellon University, Pittsburgh, Pennsylvania 15213
(Complete courses, grades 9–12, some already available from
Holt, Rinehart and Winston; no longer intended for
bright children only)
Supported in part by U.S.O.E.

Social Studies Curriculum Revision
Mildred McChesney
New York State Education Department, Albany, New York
(Social studies revision, grades K–12)
Supported by the State

University of Michigan Curriculum Project, also Michigan
Social Science Education Project
Robert S. Fox and Ronald Lippitt
College of Education, University of Michigan, Ann Arbor,
Michigan 48106

(Primarily units for elementary schools)
Supported in part by U.S.O.E.

Geography-Conservation

Conservation Education Improvement Project
  Howard M. Hennebry
  College of Education, University of Wyoming, Laramie,
    Wyoming 82070
  (Conservation education materials, grades K–9)
  Supported in part by U.S.O.E.

Curriculum Guide for Geographic Education
  National Council for Geographic Education (N.C.G.E.)
  Illinois State University, Normal, Illinois
  (Continuing interest in curriculum)
  Supported by N.C.G.E.

Elementary School Geography Project
  Charlotte Crabtree
  University of California at Los Angeles, Los Angeles, Cali-
    fornia
  (Geography, grades 1–3)
  Supported in part by U.S.O.E.

High School Geography Project
  Nicholas Helburn
  P.O. Box 1095, Boulder, Colorado 80302
  (Units and instructional materials in high school geography)
  Supported in part by the American Association of Geogra-
    phers, the Fund for the Advancement of Education, and
    the National Science Foundation

Preparation of Teaching Guides and Materials on Geography
  Louis Nicolosi
  Louisiana State Department of Education, Baton Rouge,
    Louisiana
  Supported in part by U.S.O.E.

Study of the Effectiveness of Taped Lessons in Geography Instruction
  Richard W. Elliott
  Westfield Public Schools, Westfield, Massachusetts 01085
  Supported in part by U.S.O.E.

Survey of Printed Materials on Conservation Education
  Carl S. Johnson
  Ohio State University, 1735 Neil Ave., Columbus, Ohio 43210
  (Evaluation of conservation-education materials)
  Supported in part by U.S.O.E.

Government

Center for Research and Education in American Liberties
  Columbia University, New York, New York
  Supported in part by the Ford Foundation

Council on Civil Education
  Henry Toy, Jr.
  1735 Desales St., Washington, D.C. 20036
  (Affiliated with a number of projects, civil liberties materials)
  Supported in part by the Danforth Foundation

Development of Basic Attitudes and Values toward Government and Citizenship during the Elementary School Years
  Robert D. Hess and David Easton
  Political Science Department, University of Chicago, Chicago, Illinois
  Supported by the University

Experimental Statewide Seminars in Teaching about Democracy and Totalitarianism
  Jerry Moore
  Northwestern University, Evanston, Illinois
  Supported in part by U.S.O.E.

High School Curriculum Center in Government
  Shirley Engle and Howard D. Mehlinger
  Indiana University, Bloomington, Indiana 47401
  (Teaching materials in government for grades 9 and 12)
  Supported in part by U.S.O.E.

World Law Fund
  11 West 42nd St. New York, New York 10036
  (Part of the Institute for International Order—promotes
    world law and order)
  Supported by a wide range of sources

History

Amherst Project, or Construction and the Use of Source Material Units in History and Social Studies, or The Committee on the Study of History
  Van R. Halsey and Richard Brown
  Amherst College, Amherst, Massachusetts 01002; also an
    office in the Newberry Library, Chicago, Illinois 60610
  (History materials for secondary schools)
  Supported in part by U.S.O.E.

Basic Concepts in History and Social Sciences
  Edwin Roswenc
  Department of American Studies, Amherst College, Amherst,
    Massachusetts 01002
  (Paperback books of readings published by D. C. Heath)
  Supported by the College and other sources

A Cultural Approach to the Study of History in Grades 7 and 8
  Gregory Anrig and Lawrence Vadnais, Jr.
  Mt. Greylock Regional High School, Green River Road,
    Williamstown, Massachusetts 01267
  Supported in part by U.S.O.E.

Identification of Criteria for the Effective Use of Films in Teaching History in the Classroom, in a Variety of Teaching Situations, Grades 7–12

[21]

Structure and the Social Studies

Robert L. Zangrando
American Historical Association, Washington, D.C.
Supported in part by the Association and U.S.O.E.

Service Center for History
American Historical Association
400 A St., S.E., Washington, D.C.
(Excellent summaries of scholarship on a wide variety of historical topics)
Supported in part by the Association

World History Project
L. S. Stavrianos
History Department, Northwestern University, Evanston, Illinois 60201
(Texts in world history)
Supported in part by the Carnegie Corporation

International Affairs

Asian Studies Curriculum Project or Preparation of Teaching Guides and Materials on Asian Countries for Grades 1–12
John Michaelis
College of Education, University of California, Berkeley, California 94720
(Preparation and distribution of materials on Asia)
Supported in part by U.S.O.E.

Asian Studies Project
Franklin R. Buchnan
Arps Hall, College of Education, Ohio State University, 1945 North High St., Columbus, Ohio 43210
(Clearinghouse for information related to teaching about Asia in elementary and secondary schools)
Source of support unknown

Curriculum Project on Latin America, or Development of Guidelines and Resource Materials on Latin America for Use in Grades One–Twelve

[22]

Clark Gill and William Conroy
University of Texas, Austin, Texas 78712
Supported in part by U.S.O.E.

Development and Testing of Instructional Materials, Teaching
Guides and Units on the History and Culture of Sub-Sahara
Africa, or Project Africa
Bary K. Beyer
Carnegie-Mellon University, Pittsburgh, Pennsylvania 15213
(Development of teaching materials and activities on Africa)
Supported in part by U.S.O.E.

Development of First Grade Materials on "Families in Japan"
Melvin Arnoff
405 Education Building, Kent State University, Kent, Ohio
44240
Supported in part by U.S.O.E.

Foreign Policy Association
James M. Becker
345 E. 46th St., New York, New York 10017
(A variety of materials and projects on world affairs)
Supported by many sources including U.S.O.E.

Foreign Relations Project
Jerry R. Moore
North Central Association of Colleges and Secondary Schools
    (N.C.A.), Room 740, 53 W. Jackson Blvd., Chicago,
    Illinois 60603
(Materials on foreign relations)
Supported by the Ford Foundation and the Harris Founda-
    tion

Image of Latin America: A Study of American School Text-
books and School Children Grades 2–12
Vito Perrone
Northern Michigan University, Marquette, Michigan
Supported in part by U.S.O.E.

Improving the Teaching of World Affairs
  Harold Long
  Glens Falls Public Schools, Glens Falls, New York 12801
  (Total school involvement in world affairs)
  Supported in part by the National Council for the Social
    Studies

Intercultural Studies K–16
  Wallace Anderson
  State College of Iowa, Cedar Falls, Iowa 50613
  (No data on the project available at this time)
  Supported in part by U.S.O.E.

A Study of Effectiveness of Different Methods of Teaching
International Relations to High School Students
  Dale M. Garvey and William H. Seiler
  Kansas State Teachers College, Emporia, Kansas
  Supported in part by U.S.O.E.

Survey of Asian Studies in Secondary Schools in New England
  Alan B. Cole
  Tufts University, Medford, Massachusetts
  Supported in part by U.S.O.E.

Sociology

Sociological Resources for Secondary Schools
  Robert Angell
  503 First National Building, Ann Arbor, Michigan 48108
  (Senior high school materials in sociology)
  Supported in part by the National Science Foundation

Miscellaneous

Effectiveness of using Graphic Illustrations with Social Studies
Textual Materials
  O. L. Davis, Jr.
  University of Texas, Austin, Texas
  Supported in part by U.S.O.E.

Evaluating Teaching Strategies in the Social Studies
  Milton O. Muex
  University of Utah, Salt Lake City, Utah
  Supported in part by U.S.O.E.

Materials and Activities for Teachers and Children, or Match
Box Project
  Frederick H. Krease
  Children's Museum, 60 Burroughs St., Boston, Massachusetts
    02130
  (Experimentation with teaching materials)
  Supported in part by the Museum

A Philosophical and Historical Rationale for a New Approach
to "Problems of Democracy"
  Glenn W. Hawkes
  St. Marks School of Texas, 10600 Preston Rd., Dallas, Texas
    75230
  (An analysis of American problems courses)
  Supported in part by U.S.O.E.

Social Studies Curriculum Project
  Ridgway F. Shinn
  Rhode Island College, Providence, Rhode Island 02908
  (A Study of the validity of using geography and history as
    integrating disciplines of the program, grades K–12)
  Supported in part by U.S.O.E.

Sounds of Society: A Demonstration Project in Group Inquiry
  B. J. Chandler
  Northwestern University, Evanston, Illinois
  Supported in part by U.S.O.E.

A Study of the Objectivity of Materials Used in Current Events
Instruction in Secondary School Social Studies Classrooms
  William T. Lowe
  College of Education, University of Rochester, Rochester,
    New York

(To ascertain the objectivity of current events periodicals)
Supported in part by U.S.O.E.

To Study Insights Gained from a High School Social Studies Course
   Ida Lalor and Maurice L. Hartung
   University of Chicago, Chicago, Illinois
   Supported in part by U.S.O.E.

Use of a Data Storage and Retrieval System to Teach Elementary School Children Concepts and Modes of Inquiry in the Social Sciences, or Project Star
   Bruce R. Joyce
   Teachers College, Columbia University, New York, New York 10027
   Supported in part by U.S.O.E.

All the studies listed here have some kind of outside support—foundation, government, or corporate; no attempt has been made to list studies that are operating exclusively on local funds. The range of projects included is great: Some are for single units or levels, while others are for the entire K–14 sequence; some have produced a text for a standard course in the existing curriculum, while others are interested in "starting fresh"; some are narrowly based, fairly tight empirical studies, while others lack all forms of evaluation. There is also a range in the temporal sense: some few of the studies are complete, but most are just beginning.

Foundational Ideas

A few basic ideas are common to most of these studies. In fact, it might be argued that these basic ideas provide the basis for the curriculum revision movement in all subjects.

Certainly the social studies projects, or most of them, seem to rest on common assertions, which will be briefly stated here.

1. The content of the social studies program should consist of basic questions, understandings, concepts, principles, generalizations, and methods of inquiry or processes from history, geography, and the social science disciplines. These are the components of structure. This statement does not negate the fact that scholars disagree sharply over the relative emphasis these components should receive and even on the precise meaning of the terms.

2. With this focus it would almost necessarily follow that the central aim of the program should be the intellectual development of students. There has been a clearly pronounced tendency to reject or minimize the group guidance functions of social studies that formerly had a great deal of support.

3. The ideas and methods of the historian, the geographer, and the social scientist should be organized in a sequential, ordered manner to eliminate unnecessary duplication. The term "spiral curriculum" is in vogue. Briefly, it means reinforcing an understanding of basic concepts in a variety of contexts with ever-increasing sophistication.

4. Cultural studies—human geography and cultural anthropology particularly—should receive greater attention than they have in the past. Some are saying that these areas of knowledge should serve as the organizing disciplines of the program. Economics is also demanding more time and emphasis. To a lesser degree, so are sociology and government.

5. History taught as a separate subject ought to receive less time and emphasis than it has in the past. When it is taught, more time should be spent on the recent past than was

formerly true. Also, cultural or social and intellectual history should receive greater emphasis.

6. Scholars from the contributing disciplines must be involved in curriculum decisions to a far greater degree than they have in the recent past. This direction is already well developed.

7. The so-called non-Western world and Latin America should have increased attention given to them at the expense of the time now devoted to local, regional, and national studies. International understanding is perceived by many to be a major goal.

8. Methods of inquiry are emphasized. "Inductive teaching," "discovery," "inquiry curriculum," "teaching public issues," and "critical thinking" are some of the adaptations on this theme which have been promoted.

9. Fewer topics should be taught in greater depth.

10. More abstract, more difficult, and more significant content can be taught earlier than we had supposed. "Moving down" abstractions to younger children is common.

11. "New" kinds of teaching materials, approaches, and organization plans should be emphasized: case studies, documents, readings, letters, diaries, artifacts, uninterpreted data in a variety of forms, teaming, various types of grade or nongrade organizations, programs, computers, gaming or simulation exercises, and so on.

Of these ideas or trends, our study group regarded the first, which can be called structure, as the most important. Chapter 2 will explain why.

Problems Associated with Social Studies Revision

Members of the Cornell group were enthusiastic about most of this activity. Most of us would have been delighted that something was happening at long last even if we had not agreed completely with the trends. As it was, the group was encouraged by most of the directions. We hope that our reasons will become clear. But, there are some serious problems related to curriculum revision in the social studies that should be mentioned,[11] not as criticisms of the projects under way, individually or collectively, but as discussions of the basic difficulties in doing any kind of curriculum revision in the social studies.

First is the enormous breadth of this area. Each of the social and behavioral sciences as well as history and geography offers ample content for an elementary and secondary school program. Each is expanding at a remarkable rate. These disciplines are organized in different ways and have different goals and methods of inquiry. History and geography particularly, as we shall see, are almost completely unlike the others. The problems of grouping these areas together are enormously complex. No other broad area of the curriculum—except, perhaps, general science—presents a problem of comparable difficulty. Maybe this issue will lead to an arrangement of the content into the separate fields or to a complete reorganization that would, for example, put history with the humanities. Even if this happens and is desirable, we are forced at the moment into thinking of the total study of social man as a single area of the curriculum. This organization will probably continue for some time. It is possible, of course, to think of a multidisciplinary approach as opposed to an integrated or interdisciplinary phenomenon, but either way the scope of the area is tremendous.

[11] A somewhat expanded statement of these and related issues can be found in the preface to Irving Morrissett, ed., *Concepts and Structure in the New Social Science Curricula* (New York: Holt, Rinehart and Winston, 1967).

Secondly, and probably as a direct result of this first point, there has been a decided lack of agreement regarding the purposes and priorities for teaching social studies in elementary and secondary schools.[12] How can we revise content and make any basic changes in curriculum when teachers are in sharp disagreement over what they should be trying to do? The emphasis on intellectual goals in the current curriculum projects does not entirely remove this difficulty.

As we have seen, there are groups who (1) favor intellectual goals and the structure idea; (2) focus almost exclusively on skill development; (3) want psycho-social development to be the major goal; or (4) believe attitude and value change is the only legitimate purpose. Furthermore, there are great numbers of practitioners who have never really thought about their purposes. Obviously, this split leads to difficulties in curriculum revision. One manifestation of it has been the tendency to add to the social studies any topic that seems socially significant but that no other subject area wants. Manners, orientation to the school, safety, narcotics, sex education, consumer education, vocational guidance, all of these and more, have landed on our doorstep at one time or another. State laws and requirements have contributed to this situation.

A third major problem is the controversial nature of most of the significant content in the social sciences, history, and geography. Everyone who has a position on important social, political, and economic questions has an ax to grind regarding the social studies curriculum. If something is left out, one group, at least, will surely complain. If something

[12] Some of the positions are described in Dale L. Brubaker, *Alternative Directions for the Social Studies* (Scranton, Pa.: International Textbook, 1967).

[30]

is included, pleasing some groups, others will be loudly displeased.

Finally, probably because of the other three points raised, the education of teachers in this area is tremendously difficult. The matter of scope alone creates the difficult decision of deciding whether to give future teachers a little knowledge about a broad range of topics or an understanding in depth about a limited number of subjects.

Armed with this outline of the current curriculum revision movement, let us turn to an analysis of what the study group regarded as the most important idea to emerge from the movement—the concept of structure.

[2]

Structure and Related Ideas
in the Curriculum
Revision Movement

Definition of Structure

As we have said, social studies is a late-comer to the national movement to revise the elementary and secondary school curriculum. Foreign language revision, the new math (actually the "new maths" is more accurate), the new physics, the new biology, and new chemistry, perhaps even the new English, preceded the new social studies. Chapter 1 has suggested some of the possible reasons for the revision attempts in social studies. The causes for the earlier work in other subject areas probably were similar. But no one really knows why it happened. Was it a reaction to the Progressive Era, when a good many academics were frightened away from curriculum work, was it Sputnik, the availability of money, the knowledge explosion, or was it simply scapegoating? At any rate it happened: the audio-lingual method of teaching languages developed during and right after the war, the University of Illinois Committee on School Mathematics was established in 1952, the Physical Sciences Study Committee in 1956, the chemical bond approach in 1957, the School Mathematics Study Group in 1958, the Biological Sciences Curriculum Study in 1959, and so on and on—more than a hundred national projects were in effect before the end of 1962.

In September of 1959, thirty-three scholars from a wide range of disciplines met at Woods Hole, Massachusetts, to analyze what was happening. The ten-day conference was chaired by the Harvard psychologist Jerome S. Bruner. The meeting resulted in perhaps the most important single statement concerning the curriculum revision movement—Bruner's *The Process of Education.*[1] When curriculum workers gather for meetings today, it is common to hear, "According to Saint Jerome." The remark is only partially facetious.

The Process of Education contained little that was new, since the meeting was convened primarily to assess what was already happening. However, it pulled together in one readable and concise source the underlying ideas that were and still are foundational to the revision movement. It produced a great deal of debate and soul-searching. One measure of its impact is the fact that the discussion continues to this day. I have not seen a single serious paper on curriculum in the last five years that did not include some criticism, favorable or not, of the book. The language Bruner used is widely employed in discussing the revision movement. We hear it called a "process curriculum," a "discovery curriculum," an "inquiry curriculum," an "inductive curriculum," and a "structured curriculum." We even find a distinguished spokesman on the teaching of history entitling the movement "Bruner's New Social Studies." [2] To be sure,

[1] Cambridge: Harvard University Press, 1960.
[2] Mark M. Krug, "Bruner's New Social Studies: A Critique," *Social Education,* XXX (Oct. 1966) , 400.

some of the comment has been negative. Nonetheless, the wealth of comment assures us that the movement hit a nerve somewhere.

Four major hypotheses were stated in *The Process of Education:* (1) All disciplines are reducible to fundamental and developmental ideas—that is, structure. (2) These basic ideas can be taught to almost all individuals at any age and any level of ability in some intellectually honest manner. (3) All children can develop a type of "intuitive grasp" of the nature of the disciplines that is now possessed typically only by scholars. (4) Intellectual curiosity is ample motivation for students if they are given the opportunity to think for themselves or to "discover" the structure of the disciplines; the excitement of intellectual activity or discovery is possible for everyone, and it is sufficient to motivate the student to do schoolwork. All four of these hypotheses will be briefly discussed here. The most important of the four for Bruner and for our curriculum study group is structure; consequently, it will receive most of our attention. (Actually, all four hypotheses are related and are based on structure.)

What is structure? In spite of all we have said regarding the impact of *The Process of Education,* the concept of structure is not clearly defined in the book. Bruner's later writing seems to take the reader even farther away from a precise definition.[3] He does say that the purpose of teaching is to "give a student as quickly as possible a sense of the fundamental ideas of a discipline," that "underlying principles . . . give structure to the subject," that "grasping the struc-

[3] See, for example, Jerome S. Bruner, *On Knowing: Essays for the Left Hand* (Cambridge: Harvard University Press, 1962), and *Toward a Theory of Instruction* (Cambridge: Cambridge University Press, 1966).

[34]

ture of a subject is understanding it in a way that permits many other things to be related to it meaningfully." [4] The inference then is that structure has to do with relationships among the fundamentals of a subject. Structure seems to be the fabric of fundamental ideas of a discipline and the relationships among the ideas. It is the body of ideas from a subject that must be understood if further comprehension of the field is to be obtained. This definition, of course, still leaves a lot of room for various interpretations. Ford and Pugno have said the concept of structure is "an educational expression in search of a definition." [5] A number of significant attempts have been made to refine the concept. Perhaps the most important of these have been: the National Education Association report *The Scholars Look at the Schools: A Report of the Disciplines Seminar* (Washington, D.C.: The Association, 1962) ; the Phi Delta Kappa symposium of 1963 which resulted in *Education and the Structure of Knowledge,* edited by Stanley Elam (Chicago: Rand McNally, 1964) ; Joseph Schwab's article, "The Concept of the Structure of a Discipline," *Educational Record,* XIV (July 1962) ; the Ford and Pugno volume mentioned above; Philip Phenix' *Realms of Meaning: A Philosophy of The Curriculum for General Education* (New York: McGraw-Hill, 1964) , a highly appealing work which is not in complete agreement with Bruner. In addition, there have been several recent noteworthy attempts to apply the concept or parts of it specifically to the social studies curriculum.[6]

[4] Bruner, *Process,* pp. 3, 31, 7.

[5] G. W. Ford and Lawrence Pugno, eds., *The Structure of Knowledge and the Curriculum* (Chicago: Rand McNally, 1964), p. 1.

[6] H. M. Clements and others, *Social Study: Inquiry in Elementary Classrooms* (Indianapolis: Bobbs-Merrill, 1966) ; Edwin Fenton, *Teaching the New Social Studies in Secondary Schools* (New York: Holt,

Structure and the Social Studies

This activity has helped to clarify the concept. Structure is now perceived to have two dimensions. The first comprehends those fundamental concepts, propositions, principles, generalizations, understandings, and ideas that are foundational to each discipline. The second includes the organization, methods of inquiry, and ways of approaching knowledge that are distinct (or partially so), those attributes that Bruner seems to have meant when he spoke of the developmental relations between concepts. In describing the first dimension we have deliberately ignored the semantic confusion that exists over the precise meanings of "concepts," "generalizations," and the other terms. It is true that the distinctions between some of these are important. But for our purposes, since all of them are included in structure, commonsense meanings should suffice. James Womack, in *Discovering the Structure of Social Studies,* does define the terms if the reader seeks more precision.

Bruner and most other writers on this subject have said that all disciplines have structure. In fact, they argue, structure sets the boundaries or the scope of a discipline. According to this view a discipline is an identifiable category of knowledge because it has a specific and at least partially unique subject matter and an explicit, generally accepted method and approach for discovering truth. The "rock-

Rinehart and Winston, 1966); John Gibson, *New Frontiers in the Social Studies* (Boston: Tufts University, 1964); Erling Hunt, ed., *High School Social Studies Perspectives* (Boston: Houghton Mifflin, 1962); Bruce Joyce, *Strategies for Elementary Social Science Education* (Chicago: Science Research Associates, 1965); Byron G. Massialas and C. Benjamin Cox, *Inquiry in Social Studies* (New York: McGraw-Hill, 1966); *Social Studies and the Social Sciences* (New York: Harcourt, Brace and World, 1962); G. Wesley Soward, ed., *The Social Studies: Curriculum Proposals for the Future* (Chicago: Scott, Foresman, 1963); and James G. Womack, *Discovering the Structure of Social Studies* (New York: Benziger Brothers, 1966).

bottom," fundamental ideas—both substantive and methodological—are the structure. A discipline also includes less powerful ideas and facts which are added to the structure in a developmental fashion. These ideas may be ordered in terms of their importance from those with the greatest power to explain phenomena to those with the least.

The separation of structure into conceptual and methodological aspects is artificial; the two cannot be permanently disjoined. A concept only has validity if the student knows how it was conceived and how it relates to other concepts. Methodological ideas are empty and meaningless unless the student knows something of the product of their use. Still, it seems useful to separate the two aspects for purposes of analysis.

Each discipline, then, has concepts, principles, and methods having the power to explain what we observe and experience in a particular subject of interest. Some of these ideas are more basic than others—they have more power to explain, they are fundamental to other ideas which cannot be understood without a grasp of their foundations. Studying a field of knowledge means investigating its hierarchical structure.

It would be difficult to overemphasize the fact that the ways of looking at and working with these ideas is as crucial to the discipline as are the concepts and principles themselves. Phenix puts it this way:

Representative ideas are . . . at one and the same time principles of growth and principles of simplification. They are principles of growth because the patterns they reveal prove to be reproductive of further insight, yielding more and more exemplifications of what they typify. They are principles of simplification because they provide a kind of map of the discipline that keeps one from getting lost in the details. This is a surprising fact, that an understanding of the very ideas that make a discipline fertile, causing knowledge in it to expand rapidly, is also the basis for simplifying the task of learning the discipline.[7]

According to the pioneers of the new curriculum, the modes of inquiry and thought processes in the various field of knowledge differ not only because they have different subject matter but because they strive for distinct kinds of explanation. For example, the natural scientist is looking for general laws, while the historian is trying to explain unique situations of the past. They work in different kinds of "laboratories," with different kinds of data, and must use different means of gathering, verifying, and analyzing their materials. (As we will see, this fact gets us in trouble.) Knowledge in all fields is a process as well as a product. Scholars in the same field must have some basic agreement on the procedures for knowing and discovering truth; otherwise they cannot even communicate, let alone build on the work of others. At the heart of each discipline must be certain criteria for determining valid and reliable truths, and as previously indicated, the ideas of a field have significance for a student only if he perceives the ways in which these ideas were uncovered and how they lead to "new" knowledge. "The right of a scholar to speak as an authority in his field rests on his acceptance of the canons of inquiry on which knowledge in it is created and validated." [8] And Bruner's objective is to make a scholar of each student in each subject to which he is exposed.

The notion of structure implies a pragmatic epistemology. Knowledge is relative. There is no absolute truth. Sub-

[7] *Realms of Meaning*, p. 324.   [8] *Ibid.*, p. 322.

stantive and methodological structure changes. Much misunderstanding of Bruner and his "disciples" has resulted
from the misconception that the position is founded on a
belief in a single fixed structure for each discipline. Bruner
himself is partly responsible for this confusion because of his
failure to deal directly with the issue. He speaks at times of
the structure, and the reader is given the impression that
there exists a final truth out there, available to the man who
seeks it. But, Bruner also says, "knowledge is a model *we*
construct to give meaning and structure to the regularities
in experience. The organizing ideas of any body of knowledge are *inventions* for rendering experience economical
and corrected." [9] This statement seems to say that structure
is not inherent in knowledge, but is invented by men.
Bruner also speaks of the necessity of having different structures for the same discipline in order to deal with conflicting theories which cannot be proved or disproved given our
present state of knowledge.

To be sure, Bruner is consistently vague on this point,
even in his later writings, but some of his followers are not.
Schwab and Ausubel speak of the "tentativeness," the "adequacy," and the "variety" of structures.[10] The champions
of the "new curriculum" also applaud the fact that there are
a good many approaches to the "new math" and at least
three versions of biology that are focused on distinct structures for the field. In fact, one of the most attractive aspects
of the idea of structure is that it provides a theoretical basis
for dealing with change and controversy in a field. The student recognizes, or should recognize, that as we learn more
and document or refute old theories we need to revise the
old structure or develop new ones. Bruner reminds us that

[9] Bruner, *On Knowing*, p. 120; italics mine.
[10] Elam, *Education and the Structure of Knowledge*, pp. 10, 234.

scholars do this continually. They discover something and then seek a way of fitting this observation into what is already known. Frequently, the process involves rejecting what they had formerly believed to be true. This is the process of structuring. It is dynamic and it is in an important sense personal, at least at first. It is the imperfect and unfinished product of men, not an everlasting verity.

There is one final element in this definition: structure is a pedagogical concept. A structure, the one held by the teacher, should be used initially to give meaning and organization to what the child learns. This structure should serve as a model and should show the power of a structure to give meaning and substance to what one learns. The child should be encouraged to internalize a structure, modifying the teacher's when this is justified. Bruner believes, for example, that Physical Sciences Study Committee (P.S.S.C.) physics encourages students to try their hand at structuring. The teacher must help the student to find a structure that works for him.

Rationale for Structure

Structure, then, is not only the fundamental ideas of a subject; it is also the internalized way of perceiving the logical relations between these ideas and the means of arriving at them. Bruner claims a number of advantages for a structured curriculum: Structure helps students learn what is important; it helps in retention; it fosters transfer of learning; and it helps reduce the gap between the work of scholars and what takes place in the classroom.

The first claim is based on the "principle of learning," which asserts that we understand more and, therefore, learn more if what we are learning is perceived to be logically organized. This idea has been around for a long time; in fact, it seems to be one of the few things that we can take for granted about human learning. We learn more if we can sense meaningful relations with what we already know and have experienced. We learn more if we can perceive an order and sequence.

The second claim—that of increased retention—is based on the same contention; that is, learning will be more durable if the learner perceives relations and organization. Bruner makes the commonplace observation in his essay "After John Dewey, What?" that isolated, disassociated information is not long remembered.[11] Facts and ideas learned in relation to other and more fundamental facts and ideas help us to recall both. The process of retrieving a fact is aided by an awareness of the relation of that item to basic concepts and principles.

Of course, both these claims might be equally true of a curriculum ordered on any integrating or organizing principle. Structure is just one way to capitalize on the human need for logical order. The transfer argument, however, seems more specifically tied to the idea of structure. The point is made that the "explosion of knowledge" forces us to be even more conscious of the need to teach for transfer than in the past. We cannot teach all there is to know and much of what we do teach will be quickly obsolete unless we concentrate on fundamentals and, equally important, on methods of inquiry. These change less rapidly and provide a framework for adding and amending when the situation warrants. According to those who accept the idea of structure, the best way to help students transfer what they have learned in one context to another situation outside the classroom is to teach them the basic ideas, the relationships among the ideas, or the methods of inquiry from the various

11 Bruner, *On Knowing*, p. 120.

teaching fields. In this regard Bruner and others speak of the "economic," "generative," and "regenerative" power of the idea of structure.[12] These terms refer to the efficiency and developmental, or stimulating, character of studying structural ideas.

The final claim Bruner makes for structuring the curriculum is that the gap between student and scholar, between classroom practices and scholarship, will be lessened. Students will spend their time on learning the important, exciting, and yet basic ideas, the same ones being used by men on the frontiers of scholarship, rather than on acquiring that dull, grey background of details which people have traditionally thought had to be learned prior to the act of thinking. The students start by thinking about significant ideas instead of ending there.

This, then, is the nature and defense of structure, the first of Bruner's hypotheses and the one that he regarded as the most significant of the four ideas underlying the curriculum revision movement in all fields. Before we try to assess this concept, however, we will return for a moment to the other three ideas or hypotheses that Bruner cited. As I have said, these hypotheses seem to depend on structure.

Three Related Ideas

The second of the four hypotheses is concerned with readiness—anything can be taught to anybody in some intellectually respectable way. This idea was greeted with surprise and outrage when it was first expounded. The argument seemed to reject the years of research by developmental psychologists. In fact, it seemed contrary to the very work cited by Bruner and done by the Geneva School, particularly by Piaget and Inhelder. But was it contradictory?

[12] Bruner, *Process*, p. 25.

Bruner's explanation suggests not. One of the assumptions held by many professional educators is a belief that children develop in stages—the "average" child goes through fairly predictable steps in his growth. If we know these stages, then there is a golden moment to introduce a topic, a skill, or an attitude. It was believed that in the interest of efficiency it was better to wait until the child was ready—intellectually, emotionally, experientially, and physically—for the introduction of something new.

Bruner does not deny that children get more sophisticated as they mature; in fact the whole idea of structure rests on this fact. But he also thinks that young children can and do perceive significant ideas in their own way, in their "own grammar," in their own logic systems. Basic ideas and methods—the structure of a discipline—can and should be introduced early, using the language appropriate to the stage of development of the child. The leaders of the new curriculum think that readiness has been improperly used to withhold ideas from pupils. Educators have tried to fill pupils' heads with a store of facts in the belief that connections and relationships and "big ideas" must come later. But the curriculum organization we need is one that emphasizes ideas at the beginning and then returns to the ideas again and again in different and ever more sophisticated contexts —the spiral curriculum.

Bruner accepts at least in part the stages of development that have been identified by the Geneva group of psychologists. He wants to use this information to help determine the most appropriate language and context available for introducing structure. Young children, at least most of the time, have to be introduced to ideas first through action, as opposed to abstract thinking; they have to "act out" the idea or in other ways do something with it. Setting up a store to teach economic principles is a commonplace example. Later, students may be introduced to ideas through imagery. Here, diagraming is helpful. Finally, when the child has gone through these stages, ideas can be presented through symbols, including verbal forms. Sometimes it is possible to skip a stage, but the pattern holds more often than not.

The problem is to identify the basic ideas and then place them in the language, context, stages, and "grammar" appropriate for the child. We are strongly warned of the dangers inherent in delaying this process on the grounds that students cannot comprehend the fundamentals. To document his view that students can learn significant ideas early, Bruner cites impressive but inconclusive evidence.[13] The evidence, mainly Inhelder's work, is based on research in teaching mathematics and physics. Bruner speculates that "a comparable approach can surely be taken to the teaching of social studies and literature." [14]

The third and fourth of Bruner's hypotheses are concerned with "the intuitive grasp of structure" and "discovery." Many of the leaders of the curriculum revision movement argue that the program of studies of the past has been almost exclusively organized on an analytic, formalistic basis. If thinking was desired at all in the old curriculum, then the teacher wanted analytical thinking—a formal, step-by-step, logical progression. The new curriculum ought to emphasize intuition, "the intellectual technique of arriving at plausible but tentative formulations without going through the analytical steps by which such formulations would be found to be valid or invalid conclusions." [15]

[13] Jerome S. Bruner, "Some Theorems on Instruction Illustrated with Reference to Mathematics," *Theories of Learning and Instruction,* ed. Ernest Hilgard (Chicago: University of Chicago Press, 1964), pp. 314, 329–331, and Bruner, *Process,* pp. 40, 41.

[14] Bruner, *Process,* p. 46.   [15] *Ibid.,* p. 13.

[44]

The "intuitive leap" involves insight, the apprehension of meaning suddenly and dramatically, the "ah-ha" phenomenon. The hunch, the hypothesis, and the "big picture" are placed at a premium. Again, this notion is clearly not new. The Gestalt principle was with us long before Koffka and Lewin provided language for it. Bruner's interpretation has some special twists, but these are unimportant for us here. We need only note that an underlying idea of the movement is the belief that "it [is] of first importance to establish an intuitive understanding of materials before we expose our students to more traditional and formal methods of deduction and proof." [16] The testing of hunches must come, to be sure, but later. In almost poetic style Bruner has called for more "left-handedness," dreaming, intuiting, and less "right-handedness," or formal analysis.[17] One encourages intuition by teaching structure—by raising the questions scholars are discussing and at the same time providing a stimulating, open, intellectual climate. In a fascinating way Bruner sees intuition as an end and a means, a cause and an effect of teaching structure. A teacher encourages pupils to be intuitive so that they may arrive at an understanding of structural ideas, and, in turn, the acquiring of these ideas develops intuitive powers. One begins to teach on the basis of the child's natural but undeveloped powers of insight and then develops them.

This appealing idea of intuition is, of course, itself intuitive. The deductive formal testing stage for the notion of intuition has not yet been achieved by psychologists, as Bruner knows. He admits that it is even impossible at the present time to behaviorally and precisely define intuition. Still, the appeal is there. What teacher can fail to be attracted to a position that encourages individuality, freedom,

[16] *Ibid.,* p. 59.   [17] Bruner, *On Knowing.*

[45]

and creativity and discourages dreary formalism? Think of a school in which students are motivated to discover principles and relationships among ideas with the same drive that mature scholars have. Think of a school in which teachers themselves act on intuitive hunches and are thrilled by working with ideas. Think of a school in which the intrinsic rewards of discovering structure are all the motivation that a student needs. Imagine the sheer delight of having students engaged together in first intuitive and then analytical thinking. Of course the idea has appeal. But is it an inspired fantasy? This is quite another matter and the evidence is not yet in.

The essence of the fourth hypothesis, discovery, Bruner describes as "a matter of rearranging or transforming in such a way that [the learner] is enabled to go beyond the evidence so reassembled to new insights." [18] Once again, the "discovery" idea is clearly not new. Mauritz Johnson, Jr., documents this point in an effective and witty way in "Who Discovered Discovery?" [19] But Saint Jerome must be given credit for making the word a regular part of our jargon, if not of our teaching procedures.

According to this hypothesis, teachers must employ techniques that lead pupils to find generalizations for themselves. Of course, this process cannot be attempted in every case or we would never have any progress, but the most productive learning and retention situation is the discovery one. Phenix more modestly calls the process "guided rediscovery." [20] The terms "guided" and "rediscovery" might seem like half a loaf, stopping short of the goal, for Bruner. Massialas and Cox have called their approach "inquiry-

[18] *Ibid.*, pp. 82–83.
[19] *Phi Delta Kappan,* XLVIII (Nov. 1966), 120.
[20] *Realms of Meaning,* pp. 336–337.

centered." [21] This description also suggests an affinity with Bruner, but he would probably insist on the intuitive aspect of the act of learning far more than does Massialas. A curriculum could be focused on the inquiry process and be highly formalistic. One can imagine a teacher having students recite the steps in the scientific method and then go through dull drill sessions in which one problem after another would be subjected to the formal stages. The teacher would supply the data and clarify the problem, and the students would dutifully arrive at the conclusion the teacher had expected. This may be a useful exercise, but it is not discovery-teaching in Bruner's sense. Of course, it is not what Cox and Massialas want either. The terms employed by Phenix and Massialas and Cox have only been introduced here to suggest a few of the qualifications that have been added to Bruner's ideas.

How much freedom should the child have and how much guiding or directing should the teacher do? Should the students be encouraged to discover or merely rediscover? Should they be encouraged to develop their own methods of inquiry or should the young child, particularly, be required to learn to follow traditional ways? Bruner does not hedge on these questions:

Intellectual activity anywhere is the same, whether at the frontier of knowledge or in a third-grade classroom. What a scientist does at his desk or in his laboratory, what a literary critic does in reading a poem, are of the same order as what anybody else does when he is engaged in like activities—if he is to achieve understanding. The difference is in degree, not in kind. The schoolboy learning physics *is* a physicist, and it is easier for him to learn physics behaving like a physicist

[21] *Inquiry in Social Studies.*

than doing something else. The "something else" usually involves the task of mastering . . . a "middle language"—classroom discussions and textbooks that talk about the conclusions in a field of intellectual inquiry rather than centering upon the inquiry itself.[22]

A central purpose of the curriculum for Bruner is bridging the gap between scholarship and the classroom. The way to do this is to force the schoolboy to be a scientist, a historian, an author. He must not study scholarship alone, he must do it. He must use the methods of others, and he must develop his own. In so doing he learns how to learn. This is the essence of transfer. Methods of inquiry are more durable than facts and even generalizations.

Analysis of Structure

These then are the concepts of structure and the associated ideas behind the new curriculum as a majority of our study group saw them. Obviously, we believe the new curriculum is important or this book would not have been written, but the study group did have and still does have some questions: Does the idea of structure provide a theoretical base for all of the curriculum or is it too vague and incomplete? Will the new curriculum patterned on structure and the other ideas we have identified be beneficial for social studies education? Is structure the best idea now available for ordering the curriculum? Is the idea valid in all fields?

Our answers to these questions are predicated on four basic assumptions, all of which have been voiced often enough to have become almost trite. First, the so-called "knowledge explosion" is real. History, geography, and the

[22] *Process,* p. 14.

social sciences are experiencing a remarkable growth of scholarship similar to the one that is occurring in the natural sciences, although the general public is less aware of it. All we need do to document this point is to survey the sheer bulk of the writing in these fields and compare the output with earlier periods.

Second, the traditional areas of knowledge are having an identity crisis. Almost all disciplines are going through the trying exercise of asking: What are we? What should we do? How should we do it? How do we relate to other disciplines? Fundamental questions are being raised about the nature, scope, and methods of the various disciplines. Most people took the answers to these questions for granted until a few years ago. The questions will be considered in some detail in the following chapters, but for now the reader need only keep the fact of this identity crisis in mind while reviewing our analysis of structure.

Third, the new curriculum movement is, in fact, a movement. To be sure, it is not a completely cohesive, unified development. Oliver and Shaver, for example, completely reject parts of the idea of structure.[23] Phenix, although he has been identified with the movement and wants "fundamentals" taught, is more concerned with "meaninglessness" in modern life. He is greatly troubled about a curriculum that is too academic or too dependent on the traditional disciplines. He wants the school to play an important role in an effort to improve the mental health of young people. We have already said that Cox and Massialas are more concerned with traditional analytical methods of inquiry than is Bruner. Brown at Amherst is silent on the topic of structure. Fenton clearly has reservations. Instead of developing

[23] Donald W. Oliver and James P. Shaver, *Teaching Public Issues in High School* (Boston: Houghton Mifflin, 1966).

"spirals" for kindergarten to twelfth grade, a good many of the curriculum projects are designed for one grade or even smaller units. Nor do they talk about what comes after or before their suggestions. The reformers have not organized into one group. Mark Krug, in my view the sharpest of the critics of the movement, is correct in saying in the opening sentence of his book: "Let me say with all candor that this book rests on a premise and a hope that there are vast numbers of social studies professors and social studies teachers who have serious doubts about the 'new' social studies." [24] Yet in spite of the fact that there are significant disagreements, I stand by my use of the term "movement." I believe the ideas listed in Chapter 1 are common to nearly all the projects. In short, I assume that the similarities outweigh the differences in importance, that there is substantial agreement in the new curriculum "movement."

Finally, a curriculum needs to be founded on some theory. Our study group went into the project believing this, and now we are certain of it. I have already argued that the most serious problem in the curriculum of the past was its lack of any focus, of any real purpose or direction. Having teachers who know why they are doing what they are doing is in my judgment the most important single element in successful teaching.

The idea of structure and its associated concepts do, we believe, provide a theoretical base for the curriculum. In addition, in spite of all the ambiguity surrounding the term, it seems to us that structure provides the best framework of any idea we have seen. A structured curriculum or, better, an attempt to structure the curriculum of the social sciences, history, and geography will be a big step forward.

In general, then, our enthusiasm for the concept of struc-

[24] Mark M. Krug, *History and the Social Sciences* (Waltham, Mass.: Blaisdell, 1967), p. ix.

ture as a foundation for constructing a new curriculum rests on five points:

1. Regardless of the precise definition of "structure," there can be no attempt to structure the curriculum without consulting the scholars in the various disciplines. These are the people, the only people, who can and should tell us what to teach. Educationists, school administrators, committees of otherwise overworked teachers, or textbooks should not determine what is taught. The people who know what is going on in the exploding fields of knowledge must play a dominant role in determining the subject matter of the curriculum. The elementary or secondary school classroom teacher should make the vital methodological decisions, but he must have help in deciding what to teach. Structure provides a theory that insists on the proper involvement of scholars.

2. The concept of structure necessarily gives the social studies an intellectual focus, an emphasis on fundamental ideas and methods of inquiry. Social studies instruction cannot accomplish, single-handedly, the socialization of youngsters, although in the past it has almost attempted this feat. The field must have priorities, and we believe they must be intellectual ones. The basic purpose of the school should be the intellectual development of its clients, and social studies should and must be a part of this goal. For the interested reader, the writer and his colleagues have developed this idea in detail elsewhere.[25] Suffice it to say here that we applaud the notion of structure partially because it provides a sorely needed intellectual orientation for the social studies.

3. Closely related to this point is the argument that struc-

[25] Mauritz Johnson, Jr., Gordon F. Vars, William T. Lowe, and Oscar G. Mink, *Intellectual Purposes of the Junior High School* (Ithaca, N.Y.: Junior High School Project, Cornell University, 1967).

ture does provide a means of teaching for transfer to non-classroom situations. Methods of inquiry and fundamental ideas have more permanence and, therefore, much more transferability than isolated facts or even generalizations.

4. Likewise, structure provides a rationale for moving significant intellectual content into the lower levels of the educational program. Our group was convinced that elementary school youngsters, or most of them, can handle more abstractions and more significant ideas than they have previously been exposed to.

5. Finally, structure and its associated ideas suggest a method of teaching that is consistent with what we know about human learning. Active involvement of students; the development of a love of learning, of a strong desire to know; and the importance of perceiving relationships and organization have a carefully documented association with learning and retention. Structure insists on these conditions.

In spite of all we have said, there are some problems—some of them so serious that they cast doubt on the validity of the idea at least in certain fields. What are these problems? At the heart of the difficulty, as we have noted throughout, is the fuzziness of the concepts. Discovery, intuition, and structure are not precise, analytic concepts—perhaps they never will be. But we need to try to sharpen them if they are to give specific directions. In addition, there is little research evidence to document many of the assertions of Bruner and his associates. The teachers I have talked to who have tried some of the structured materials feel that they work well, but we certainly have no empirical evidence that more learning takes place, that more is retained, or that transfer is better facilitated. How young is too young to introduce abstractions? We don't know. Precisely how much discovery is possible and desirable? We don't know. What is the correct balance between various modes of thinking—analysis and intuition? We don't know. Then there is the potential problem that we have already mentioned, namely that proponents of the idea will in spite of all the warnings be satisfied to develop a single structure, a single curriculum. Bruner, as we said before, gives comfort at points to this one-structure-out-there, way of thinking. But if a discipline ever became convinced that it had found its one, unchanging structure, it would be literally dead. Nevertheless, this is a potential problem.

Furthermore, if we have a structured curriculum, then some things we are now teaching will be omitted. Will the pressures on the school permit leaving things out? Economic and ideological interest groups want their stories told. External examinations and a host of other pressures exist. The scholar in his ivory tower is not free to determine what we teach. Public schools under our existing set-up must be subject to the influences of community forces. Can these forces and a structured curriculum live together?

Another problem is the matter of selection. Once we decide to use the structure idea, we are still left with the problem of making decisions about which structure to teach—they cannot all be taught. How does one decide?

Finally, and by far most important in our view—Is structure a valid idea in some fields but not in others? Do the humanistic and aesthetic areas defy the notion of structure? Is art, for example, so individualistic, so introspective that the idea of structure is not appropriate? Returning to the disciplines being studied here, the next chapter will deal with this question as it relates to history. The issue, again, is: Is it possible to identify structure in a field such as mathematics and to teach children to think like mathematicians, but impossible and/or undesirable to achieve this same end in history?

[3]

History

The historians who worked with our study group were Professor Donald Kagan, Professor Edward Fox, and Professor Walter LaFeber, all distinguished Cornell faculty members. Unlike our other consultants, they did not attempt to define their discipline or examine its form. They did not discuss in detail the nature of history or historical method; nor did they discuss their views on the relevance of our notion of structure to the discipline. I would hypothesize that at least two of them would reject outright the idea of structure as the basis for determining the history curriculum. To be sure, they believe that history should be taught to all children (their specific suggestions about what topics should be taught are outlined in the final section of this chapter). They believe fundamental ideas should be emphasized. But they would not, I think, accept the hierarchical nature of concepts and the emphasis on methods of inquiry which we have argued are essential to a structured curriculum. Professor Fox, for example, said he did not feel that children should be taught how the historian works. Historiography, according to Fox, is for graduate students and professional historians. Attempting to teach young children to think like historians "might well kill the romantic appeal of the narrative of history."

Why did these historians take this view? Partial answers may be obtained from the literature of historiography and the philosophy of history.

Nature and Uses of History

What is history? is an age-old question, and there is a tremendous literature on the subject. As Page Smith observes, "The problem of the nature and meaning of history has been one of the most persistent riddles with which man has concerned himself once he advanced beyond the level of primitive. [Yet] the study and writing of history [is] one of the principal means by which man has extended his understanding of himself and his strange destiny." [1] In spite of the hoary nature of the problem, and in spite of the fact that there has been a lot written about the topic, few practicing historians and particularly American historians have made any systematic attempts to study the problems of doing history. They have had little to say about methodological problems. There have been a fairly large number of philosophers, on the other hand, who have written on this subject.

In the past, historians and philosophers of history have had little patience with each other. Historians, like most scholars, are interested in getting on with the job, while philosophers have been interested in studying the meaning of history and the process of doing it. There is, of course, nothing unique about this situation. The division exists in all fields between practitioners and theoreticians. Still, the dichotomy has seemed particularly pronounced in history. In recent times, however, more and more scholars from

[1] *The Historian and History* (New York: Knopf, 1964), pp. 3, 4.

both groups have spoken of the need to try to resolve their differences or at least to communicate with each other. One bit of evidence for this development was the creation of a new journal, *History and Theory;* [2] another was the occurrence in 1962 of a national symposium of historians interested in historiography and philosophers interested in the meaning of history.[3]

What do active historians think of their field? When asked, how do they describe what they do with their professional lives? In spite of the claim that historians, by and large, have not done a lot of writing about the nature of their field, a good many have at least written definitions. In one of the briefest and best, Professor Robert Daniels says that "history is the memory of human group experience." [4] Henry Steele Commager defines history as "the total record of the past—literature, law, architecture, social institutions, religion, philosophy, all indeed that lives in and through the memory of man. . . . But memory, as we all know, is fitful and phantasmagoric. History is organized memory, and the organization is all important." [5] Nearly all historians I have read would add a contemporary element to Commager's statement. Eric Kahler says, "History reflects the development of human consciousness, of man's awareness of himself." [6] He means living men. He argues that if history does not help to give modern man a sense of identity

[2] *History and Theory: Studies in the Philosophy of History,* published in The Hague by Mouton.

[3] A book resulted: Sidney Hook, ed., *Philosophy and History* (New York: New York University Press, 1963).

[4] *Studying History: How and Why* (Englewood Cliffs, N.J.: Prentice-Hall, 1966), p. 3.

[5] *The Nature and the Study of History* (Columbus, Ohio: Merrill, 1965), p. 3.

[6] Erich Kahler, *The Meaning of History* (New York: Braziller, 1964), p. 27.

and meaning, then it is not worthy of study. Page Smith has put it this way: "Selfhood, or identity, or authenticity is only achieved when larger dimensions are opened to the individual—the community, the nation, mankind, the transcendent history." [7] Our study has led to this statement: History is the carefully organized and selected record of all aspects of man's past which should help us to understand both our predecessors and ourselves. Probably most practicing historians could accept this statement. But the definition is vague, to say the least.

It does say that history has utility. This is not to claim that history repeats itself, or that its "lessons" are "laws"; but it does purport to give meaning and understanding to human activity. Some historians have tried to be more specific, and some are almost poetic about its goals. Commager claims that it "fires the imagination, broadens intellectual horizons and deepens sympathies." [8] He believes that history helps to temper our natural parochialism and helps to give us patience and tolerance. Others argue that it provides a sense of humility and, at the same time, an optimism by showing that purposeful men can affect their destinies. Daniels says that history provides an ideal vehicle for teaching men to think independently:

Historical study requires constant exercise in the relationship of details and generalizations. It gives experience in the organization and classification of extensive data. It teaches the student how to look for relevant information and to use it in solving problems. If you approach it right, history teaches you how not to be swamped by details that will soon be forgotten, but to use them in order to develop understanding.[9]

[7] *Historian and History,* p. 246. [8] *Nature and Study,* p. 92.
[9] *Studying History,* p. 7.

Daniels goes on to argue that the subjective aspect of history
—the inevitable bias of the historian—makes the discipline
particularly fruitful for teaching people how to think. He
says that since the role of individual opinions, values, and
imagination is a crucial one, history encourages individuality and creativity. Some historians claim that history can
serve in the same way that religion, theology, and philosophy do for some—to give students personal guidelines to
help them cope with life.

Methods of History

In *Understanding History,* Louis Gottschalk makes the
work of the historian sound rather simple in spite of the
mystique that we tend to associate with the field. Most of
the book is devoted to a discussion of the outline of historical method that I will quote, but for our purposes this outline and a few explanatory comments will suffice. Gottschalk
says that once a historian has selected the place, period, set
of events, institution, or men he wants to study, his job re-
duces itself to four essentials:

(1) the collection of the surviving objects and of the printed,
written, and oral materials that may be relevant; (2) the exclu-
sion of those materials (or parts thereof) that are unauthentic;
(3) the extraction from the authentic material of testimony
that is credible; (4) the organization of that reliable testimony
into meaningful narrative or exposition.[10]

So the historian picks a subject, acquires data, validates the
evidence, and tells his story. In the data-gathering stage he is
interested in artifacts—coins, stamps, tools, potsherds, and
other materials. He is also interested in talking to people

[10] *Understanding History: A Primer of Historical Method* (New
York: Knopf, 1963) , p. 28.

who have experienced something that may have relevance for him. There are, of course, more or less sophisticated techniques of interviewing, for example, or working with artifacts, and the historian needs to be as knowledgeable about these procedures as possible. But most of the historian's work is with written materials. He must develop skills in knowing where and how to find sources, but, most important, he must be a critical reader. Historians must read primary materials with great care and secondary materials with even greater care. They must read public papers, private papers, diaries, newspapers, memoirs, biographies, government documents, poetry, fiction, letters, official records, in short, everything that may be relevant.

Having gathered his data, the historian must authenticate his sources. This process is what the historian calls "external criticism." Is the document genuine? Was it written at the appropriate time? In short, is the source as a whole what it purports to be? At this point the historian uses a variety of procedures including logical and chemical tests. He uses the means and skills of the semanticist, the archaeologist, the genealogist, the chronologist, the philologist, and so on and on.

He now turns to "internal criticism." He asks such questions as: Do the witnesses agree? Is there contradictory evidence? Did the writer actually observe what happened? How much time elapsed between the event and the writing? What was the writer's purpose? For whom was he writing? Did he have the ability and the desire to tell the truth? What was his frame of reference? What was the nature and extent of his involvement in the event? Is there any corroboration for his view? During this phase, the historian uses logical methods to try to determine the accuracy, relevance, inclusiveness, balance, consistency, documentability, in short, the objectivity of his sources. Through this stage, his methods may have been similar to those of the social scientist.

Once the historian has authentic and valid sources (and he must have considered all the sources available to him) he is in a position to tell his story. He must, of course, try to tell the story honestly and fairly; historical "objectivity" demands that his assumptions and biases must be made explicit. But more is also required. The writing of history, good history, makes sophisticated demands involving style, organization, selection, intuition, generalization, synthesis, and explanation.

It is at this point that the problems for our study arise. Most contemporary historians admit that they have no explicit methodology for performing this final activity. In fact, they say that they cannot even describe what they do. Depending on their point of view, they claim that what goes on in the historian's mind is either a mystery or common sense, and that this is the way the situation will probably remain. Psychology, analytic philosophy, perhaps even zetetics, may provide some answers regarding the writing of history in the future, but they have not so far. Most historians apparently think it is futile to try to be very specific about this process. Leo Gershoy attempted to describe what he did in his biographical work on the period of the French Revolution, but he failed to provide more than a description of his personal and highly complex thought patterns.[11] He did not provide specific guidelines for other historians to follow, nor did he really try to accomplish this goal. The writing and synthesis of historical scholarship is at the heart of

[11] "Some Problems of the Working Historian," in Hook, *Philosophy and History*, p. 59.

doing good history, but historians are loath to assign any particular expertise to the task. Commager says:

There is no formula for historical writing. There are no special requirements, except the technique of writing clearly and the requirements of honesty and common sense. It is useful to have special training for almost anything you wish to do well —driving a car, or cooking, or painting—but special training is by no means essential, and most of the great historians have been innocent of formal training. . . . Integrity, industry, imagination, and common sense—these are the important, indeed essential requirements.[12]

He does not try to explain what the nature of the special training would be if the student wanted it; however, one gets the impression that it would consist of a trial-and-error period of writing history under the supervision of an experienced historian. This problem of training will be discussed later in the chapter. First, we should consider another element of the nature of history—organization.

Organization

The primary dimension of history is time. Consequently, historians organize their subject into periods, eras, epochs, centuries, decades, lifetimes, and so forth. Yet historians tend to agree that some of the standard time divisions make little sense and a few of them are centers of controversy, "middle ages," for instance, or "modern times." There is an interesting literature on periodization in history. It focuses on why and where and how to make the divisions, and it suggests that dividing events into periods of time is a necessary evil. Continuities, after all, are frequently more signifi-

---

[12] *Nature and Study,* p. 37.

cant in understanding men than are discontinuities. Furthermore, few if any single dates in history have markedly changed men in any basic sense. Nevertheless, Periodization seems to be a necessary tool for dealing with the scope of the field, and the student of history must accept some time divisions, albeit with reservations and qualifications.

History is also subdivided by place or physical location. Local community, regional, multinational, and, most important, national histories exist. Consequently, the threat of provincial bias is ever present. Historians seem to agree that this is just another inevitable potential danger of writing and reading history. Most college departments of history are organized on the basis of a curious combination of time and place factors. There is little agreement about a "best plan" for organizing the field.

At times social or cultural factors are used to divide history. We use the term "civilization" to broaden the scope from nationalities. Social institutions or value systems are sometimes used to delimit a group for study, but, in both political and social histories time still provides the basic organizational framework. All aspects of the nation or culture or group are studied in a chronological order.

Sometimes a study of the totality of life is not the goal. Instead, certain topics are chosen for study in isolation or semi-isolation from other aspects. The most commonly selected divisions are political, economic, military, diplomatic, cultural, social, and intellectual. Almost every conceivable subdivision of these broad areas has been used.

The final means of dividing history that I will mention is the biographical one. A man or a man and his family are used to organize history on occasion. (It has frequently been argued that this type of history makes the most sense for young children.)

Historians caution against overspecialization in any of these areas. While they are aware that it is necessary to divide the scholarly task, they continually remind us that happenings in one aspect of life necessarily affect developments in all others. Historians want partial interpretations or topical histories to be plainly labeled for what they are. They want every historian to be a generalist first and then a specialist.

There are, of course, many variations on these basic organizational patterns. The "flashback" is one example. But most historians are suspicious of nonchronological approaches.

The Unique Character of History

Obviously, each of the disciplines included in this report is in one way or another unique; but history and to a lesser degree geography are "more unique" than the others. These two fields cannot be grouped by any meaningful criteria with any other areas of knowledge. As we will see, I do not include geography with the social sciences because it is more than a social science. However, geography does have goals and procedures which are consistent with the behavioral sciences, indeed with all the sciences. History, on the other hand, both borrows from and contributes to the sciences, but it is not itself a division of science. Neither is it exclusively a branch of the arts or the humanities. Its distinct way of looking at man sets it completely apart, and its distinctiveness presents special problems for the curriculum worker and, particularly, for the curriculum worker enamored of the idea of structure. How is history different from other fields and, specifically, how is it nonscientific?

All the areas of scholarship that are labeled scientific are primarily interested in the general. They seek to explain broadly the phenomena of nature. The sciences look for general laws, and they wish to predict what will happen under certain conditions. They search mainly for "if-then" propositions. Scientific research must be repeatable and its results publicly verifiable. The researcher in the sciences must be imaginative and creative in his thinking and planning, but his results must not be dependent on his personality. Any fellow scientist following his procedures must get the same results. His values will influence his choice of subject matter and to some extent his procedures, but his results must not be contaminated by those values. His analytic tools or concepts must be sharp and clear, at least to his colleagues. If they are not, he must try to make them so before he uses them. His hypotheses must be universally true— must hold up in all cases—or they must be rejected. The scientist is usually trying to see the similarities between phenomena. Science is almost always recorded in formal abstractions and symbols—a separate technical language for each branch. It is supposed to be artifical in the sense of being removed from emotions and human realities.

Now, to be sure, scientists would undoubtedly quibble with some of the details of this description of their work, but nearly all of them would probably agree to the substance. Historians, to the contrary, would not accept any of these conditions for their field. History simply does not fit this scientific model, and most historians, the overwhelming majority of them in our day, are quite willing to accept this state of affairs. "Historians and philosophers seem to agree by now that history is not a science and has nothing to do with science." [13] As we shall see, I think this statement goes too far, for history does have a close communion with science; but this type of remark is common in the literature on the subject.

[13] Kahler, *Meaning of History*, p. 188.

[64]

It is true that there have been and continue to be some historians and a good many philosophers of history who claim that history can be and should be as scientific as any other discipline, or at least as scientific as any field interested in studying social man. Leopold van Ranke, a nineteenth-century German historian, is probably the most important single figure in the movement in recent times to make history a scientific study. As usual, some of his disciples went much farther in demanding hard empirical or scientific tests of historical scholarship than he did. In the twentieth century Karl Popper, C. G. Hemple, and others of the "positivist" school have argued for placing history among the scientific disciplines.

The opposite of the positivist view has been called the idealistic one. This position had been led in modern times by Wilhelm Dilthey and later by Benedotto Croce, Ortega y Gasset, and R. G. Collingwood. There are significant differences among the men I have grouped into each of the two camps, but this simplistic dichotomy—idealist versus positivist—will suffice for our purposes. As I have already implied, most historians have ignored the debates between these camps, and, indeed, they seem to be oblivious to any of the other philosophical arguments, such as the vigorous existential movements of the twentieth century. Practicing historians, however, or most of them, are idealists whether they know it or not. For this reason, it may be useful to identify in an admittedly oversimplified way some of the differences between the positivists and the idealists or between the "objectivists" and the "subjectivists."

The idealist begins his argument with the assumption that the peculiarities of both the subject matter and the goals of history are such that historical knowledge necessarily has a logic and a basic organization that is different from all other areas of knowledge. History, therefore, cannot be classified with any other field, and, of greater importance, the tests of validity and reliability of other fields are not appropriate for history. Positivists, on the other hand, say that history ought to have and can have the same logical structure as other disciplines. The scientific method with a few modifications is as appropriate for history as for any other field. If this were not so, there would be nothing worthy of the name "historical knowledge." Idealists say that history is what historians do and have done, and what historians do is decidedly personal, individualistic, interpretive, introspective, and clearly humanistic and artistic. Positivists admit that much of what passes as historical scholarship is really literature, but they want history to be what historians *ought to do*. Historians, they argue, ought to be (and can be) objective and reliable—in short, scientific. In response, idealists say that if the positivist model were followed, history would no longer be history. The field would become, at best, a social science; but more likely it would not be a discipline at all. If one assumes for the moment that it is possible to be scientific or to know assuredly about past events, then the positivist's desire would make history merely a chronicle of what happened when. According to the idealist the heart and soul of history is the stage beyond the discovery of "facts" about the past. It is the interpreting, the explaining, the generalizing, the synthesizing, the imagining, the creating, and the intuiting that matters. In short, most historians think that history is worthy of study partly because it is a unique combination of art and science.

It should be made clear that the idealist does not accept the basic assumption of the positivist that it is possible, let alone desirable, to know the "facts" of history. Events of the past cannot be verified in the present. There are too many variables over which the scholar has no control. He cannot recreate the past; he cannot replicate the conditions, the totality of life which existed at the time the event occurred. Therefore, scientific verification is not possible. Charles Beard, one of the relatively few American historians who has written and thought extensively in the field of historiography, put the situation as baldly as it can be put: "History as it actually was is not known and cannot be known." [14] Some historians of the idealist camp say that it is possible in some instances, particularly in recent history, to know historical "fact" as long as the historian is engaged in microhistory—working with a distinct, entirely separate event over a short period of time. But, they argue, when doing macrohistory—studying trends and issues, the totality of life over a long period, even a recent one—it is not possible to know the "facts" of history, nor is it desirable to be terribly concerned with trying to know them. These same historians argue that macrohistory is far more important than microhistory.

The subjectivist (idealist) believes that the point of view of the historian must color every stage in the process of doing history. When a historian selects a topic for study, when he decides which sources are credible, when he determines which "facts" to include in his story, when he selects the language and emphasis to use, when he selects hypotheses to test, when he attempts explanation, when he does all these things, he is subjective. It is necessary to go through the steps just identified, and it is equally necessary for the historian to be subjective. Subjectivity gives history its meaning and worth. The historian must view the "evidence" on his subject from his own orientation, with his personal, philosophical, social, and political biases. In fact:

[14] *The Discussion of Human Affairs* (New York: Macmillan, 1936), p. 87.

The work of the historian, like that of the artist, may be thought to be in some sense an expression of his personality. . . . The artist . . . is not content only to have and express his emotions; he wants also to communicate what he takes to be a certain vision or insight into the nature of things.[15]

The idealist believes that values and value judgments belong in history, *must* be in history—not only the values of the subjects under study, but also the values of the historian.

Yet we must avoid giving the impression that the subjectivist historian is not interested in explaining. He is. All historians want to explain some event or activity, and they regard their basic goal of understanding man to be inextricably tied to the process of explanation. Obviously, also, the idealist historian wants to be honest and accurate. He wants to answer questions such as: Why did it happen? How could it have happened? What did X have to do with it? But the idealist has been unable or unwilling to be specific about what he does when he tries to answer these questions. There have been a few attempts, in my view unsatisfactory ones, to describe the process of historical scholarship from the view of the subjectivist. In this regard some historiographers have spoken of the "perspective view." A good many active historians, consciously or not, hold this view, which states that since objectivity in history is not possible in the scientific sense for the reasons we have already identified, the best we can do, and this is good enough, is to be consistent in our biases. An historian is "objective" if he looks at all the available data and then writes his history so that all

15 W. H. Walsh, *Philosophy of History: An Introduction* (New York: Harper, 1951), p. 21.

the facts that he thinks are relevant are accounted for by the synthesis or explanation the writer presents. His report must be consistent with his point of view. It is up to the student of history then to read various accounts written from many views and draw his own conclusions in cases where the stories conflict. "Objectivity" for the historian does not mean "value-free," nor does it mean that there is a single way of truth; in history, objectivity means a logical, consistent path from the assumptions given by the historian, through his analysis of the "facts" and the conclusions he draws. As David Potter says, "The real choice is between the conscious application of reasoned and stated assumptions and the unconscious application of unreasoned and unrecognized assumptions." [16]

The positivist will not accept this limited notion of objectivity. Starting from the assumption that all empirical knowledge has the same form or logic and that history is a special case of empirical knowledge, the objectivist insists that historical explanations must be based on some verifiable "law" or "law-like" generalization. The "law" is an absolutely necessary condition of an explanation. To be sure, the positivist is willing to hedge a bit on the nature of the "law"; for example, he is frequently willing to accept a "probabilistic law," one that is usually but not universally true. He is willing to accept such qualifiers as "normally true" and "true under certain *necessary* conditions," but these conditions are not sufficient ones. That is, they would not force an event to occur. However, the positivist will not

[16] "Explicit Data and Implicit Assumptions," in Louis Gottschalk, ed., *Generalizations in the Writing of History: A Report of the Committee on Historical Analysis of the Social Science Research Council* (Chicago: University of Chicago Press, 1963), p. 183.

abandon his search for the "covering law," and he will not call a piece of writing history unless the historian has identified a "law" that he believes to be true.

The idealist denies the existence of general laws, and he denies the validity of looking for them. Historical cause, historical principles, and generalizations are a product of the reasoned judgments of the historian. As we have seen, the idealist argues that the analysis of the judgment, of the rational processes of the historian, is too complex, too involved, and too personal to be meaningfully and productively pursued. Trying to understand the stages of the thought process that an historian has completed after his work is done may be a useful and illuminating exercise, but trying to set up a model for this process before the historian works is stultifying and useless.

Implied throughout this discussion is a fact that both positivists and idealists accept: history does not have at this time sharp analytic concepts. With increasing frequency historians borrow heavily and usefully from the social sciences. They also manufacture concepts for a particular work, and then abandon them. But they do not have commonly accepted meanings for the terms they work with continually. "Motive," "cause," "influence," "power," "result," "explanation," even "fact" and "evidence," have no precise meaning that exists beyond the writing of a specific piece of history. Positivists decry this situation and want to overcome it; idealists may bemoan the situation, but recognize it as a necessary part of the craft. Historians develop generalistic causal theories from time to time—"frontier theses," "abundance," "capitalism and agrarianism"—but the majority of them return to multicausation and particularistic positions. They employ "everyday" language, and they sincerely believe in "everyman his own historian."

In summary, history according to most practicing historians is not a science. Its methods are not fully explicit. Its concerns are with particular instances and not general ones. It cannot predict and does not want to try. Its hypotheses are guides for thought for a single case. It does not have analytic concepts.

Structure and History

If this is history, does it have, can it have structure? The answer seems to be No. History as it is conceived by the majority of working historians is too loose to have structure.

In the discussion of structure in Chapter 1, we saw that structure has two intertwined aspects—the methodological and the substantive. It was asserted that while we may for analytic purposes think of the two separately, the substantive and the methodological ideas in practice are so integrated and compounded that we cannot understand one without the other. Ideas only have meaning if one knows how they are verified and validated. When methodological changes of a significant order are introduced into a dicipline, a reconsideration of concepts and generalizations should occur. Conversely, the addition of or a change in the concepts and theories of a field automatically suggests questions about methods of inquiry. Bruner's discussion of structure does not mention the methodological phase per se, but it emphasized the relations between developmental ideas. If a discipline has no explicit methodology for the bulk of its work and if it does not want such an arrangement, then it cannot have structure. If history is basically personal, individualistic, and empathetic, then it doesn't have structure. If the men and women who do history say that this state of affairs is desirable as well as the only way possible, then the "outsiders," that is, nonhistorians, including Bruner, should not try to impose structure on the field. When I deny structure in history on these grounds, I am also denying structure in all nonscientific fields. I do not think there is a structure to art or literature, beyond some very elementary principles having to do with form, color, line, mood, and so forth. Bruner and other leaders of the "new curriculum" in social studies flatly disagree with me, but so it must be.

I think some people who are anxious to give history a structure have done so by making one or both of these contentions:

1. History does not have an explicit methodology now, but it may have in the future. Furthermore, historians ought to be working toward this goal. Forcing the idea of structure on historians will help to achieve this end.

2. Structure is a feasible idea in history if we assume that there are as many structures as there are practicing historians with differing views. After all, we have consistently argued that there was no single structure "out there" waiting to be discovered. Why not argue that there are as many structures as we need to take into account every point of view in history? The curriculum then could be built on any of these structures, depending on which historian you read.

If we accept one or both of these assertions, then the notion of structure is simply not helpful anymore. If we do not know what it is and only hope it will come some day, how can we base a curriculum on it now? If it provides no more of a guide than to suggest that "anything goes," how can we use it to help us decide what to teach and what to omit?

Edwin Fenton's book on the new social studies [17] suggests that structure has meant one of three things to social studies curriculum project directors: lists of basic generalizations,

[17] *The New Social Studies* (New York: Holt, Rinehart and Winston, 1967).

lists of basic concepts, or lists of analytical questions. If any one of these is all that structure is, then history can have structure; but we have said that structure means more than a list of anything. Structure is developmental and hierarchical ideas. These related ideas must be solid enough to have the support of a good many scholars in the field. History doesn't meet these tests.

Odd as it may seem, in view of what has just been said, I believe it would be valuable for historians and curriculum workers to continue to try to accommodate the idea of structure with the prevalent view of the nature of history. This process cannot help but make us more aware of the methodological problems of history and at the same time focus our attention on the fundamental ideas of this or that historian and not on trivial details. I do not mean by awareness a desire "to reform" history, for I have no interest in and see no reason for reforming the discipline. But looking for structure may help to reduce the duplication in the existing history curriculum, and it may lead to a greater involvement of students in classroom activities. It may also help to lessen the historical orientation of the social studies curriculum and encourage a more cultural and behavioral approach. The reader is undoubtedly aware by this time that such a change would delight the writer. I am not antihistory; rather I am intrigued by it. I think it should be taught, but I think in the past it has been taught too early, too much, and too uncritically, at the expense of the social sciences. To repeat, history would have to be altered drastically to accommodate a structured curriculum, but playing with the idea of structure as it relates to the history curriculum is indeed a valuable intellectual exercise.

Historical Content to Be Taught

In view of the impracticality and imprudence of attempting to structure history, the three distinguished historians who acted as consultants for our study group devoted most of their comments to identifying key ideas from their particular specializations that should be taught to all youngsters. Professor Donald Kagan represented ancient and medieval history; Professor Edward Fox, modern European history; and Professor Walter LaFeber, American history. Their recommendations will be outlined below.

Before we examine these suggestions, however, we should perhaps consider the common assumptions on which they are based. To be sure, our consultants disagreed on some issues, but their points of agreement were greater and seem more significant for understanding the content suggestions.

Kagan, Fox, and LaFeber agree that history should be taught to all students at one or more places in the kindergarten to twelfth grade curriculum. As would be expected, they are disturbed over the apparent trend to de-emphasize history. They believe that in the high school, students should be required to take at least two years of the subject—a two-year course in western civilization including American history or separate offerings in American and European history. They do not want the western civilization course to be called "world history," and this is not just a quibble over a name. They do not believe in a survey of all history for young students. In fact, Fox argues that world history, even for graduate students and professional historians, simply does not exist. He points out that Toynbee and others have been trying to write world history, but that it has yet to be written. In addition, although our three consultants seemed to appreciate the reasons behind the demand for so-called nonwestern history, they believe it would be a serious mistake to let a course in African history, for example, steal time from the history of the Mediterranean and North Atlantic civilizations. They believe that students must have a solid grounding in their own heritage first.

They also believe that history should always be taught, at least in the precollege curriculum, in a chronological framework. The problem of what to teach should be resolved by choosing the most significant of the themes or movements, "big sweeping ideas," that have shaped western civilization. Much detail and many historical examples will have to be omitted, but the omission is not serious as long as the ideas are taught in some significant historical context. Finally, all three scholars emphatically regard history as a humanistic study and not a social science. These are the assumptions that should be kept in mind as we examine the specific concepts and contexts that the consultants suggested.

Premodern History

Professor Kagan would not begin the study of premodern history in the conventional way—a survey of prehistory and the river valley civilizations—but rather with a detailed study of ancient Greece. Four major aspects would be emphasized: the development of various types of governmental forms; the ways in which physical geography affected the development of Hellenistic civilization; the strategy, rationale, and effects of war on the society; and the significance of religion in the lives of various classes of men. Of these four aspects, Kagan believes that political history is the most important. He thinks that Greece presents an ideal context for study of the various kinds of governmental forms. The primary goal is for students to understand that men have devised a number of types and arrangements for governing themselves and that the most significant criterion for categorizing these forms is the status and role assigned to the mass of individuals. Students will study the conditions that seem to foster one kind of government as opposed to another. Kagan would mention earlier civilizations only by way of contrast.

The second major unit of study would be the Roman Empire. Again, particular elements of political, social, and military history would be emphasized. It is interesting to note that when one of the participants in the discussion questioned the emphasis on military history, Kagan emphatically argued that the role of military history has been "played down" far too much. He insisted that in spite of our feelings about the matter, war has been a highly important phenomenon in the history of western man. We must try to understand it, and this means spending time on battles and military leaders. Furthermore, the study of warfare is likely to interest students, and this interest can be used to motivate study in other aspects of history. Military history in this case should center on two phases of Roman civilization: the Punic wars and the part played in the downfall of Rome by the Germanic peoples. The political history of this unit should be focused on the Roman constitution and on the empire form of government. The social and intellectual history should trace the rise of Christianity. Students should examine the question: Why did Christianity succeed while many other religions have failed?

The third unit should center on the political and social developments of the period of western history between the decline of Rome and modern times. We might use the problem of naming the period as a gimmick to arouse interest. That is, the student could come to realize that both "Dark Ages" and "Middle Ages" are inappropriate terms. Both are prejudicial, for the period was neither dark nor merely a bridge. Teachers should ask: Why do these names persist? What better names have been suggested? Kagan believes that there is an inordinate amount of ignorance and prejudice regarding this period: "The average non-Catholic doesn't know a thing about the period; the average Catholic only knows the wrong things." What is important for people to know about the period? Three topics should be emphasized. First would be the splintering of Rome. Why did some combinations work and others fail? What was lost and what was gained for the average man, the churchman, and the scholar? The second topic would be the beginnings of French national history. How did it happen? Who were the leaders? Why? Third would be feudalism and the manorial system. How did the people live? What is the significance of the distinction between slave and serf? What was the "ultimate right" of individuals? How was the church related to the social system? What was the relation between military power and economic power? What role did the knight play —are there any parallels with earlier or later history? How did the town man become the "man in the middle"? How and why did the idea of parliament develop? What was the significance of Arab culture during this period? How did technological change affect social change? Feudalism as a political, economic, and social system should receive a great deal of attention.

The fourth and final unit of the course would be Renaissance. Students should also question the appropriateness of this term. Is Renaissance thought significantly different from scholastic thought? Did a "rebirth" occur? The majority of time should be spent on the beginnings of national monarchies, concentrating on France.

Structure and the Social Studies

Modern History

On the subject of modern European history, Professor Fox presented a stimulating defense of the best of traditional chronological surveys of modern European history. Consequently, we may summarize his remarks more briefly. He recommended six major topics: (1) The expansion of Europe—discovery, exploration, imperialism, and the importance of the idea of frontier; (2) the reformation of religions; (3) the development of national states in the modern sense—political revolutions; (4) the development of personal freedoms—social revolution; (5) industrial and economic revolution; and (6) enlightenment—intellectual revolution. Fox would end the history phase of the course with the dawn of the twentieth century, but he would spend some time on contemporary affairs from a social science point of view. He would also make comparisons and applications throughout the history course to current problems.

American History

Professor LaFeber suggested five criteria by which he would judge what to teach in American history courses. "First, I would ask what are the central strands in the American experience; words such as conflict, democracy, sectionalism, belief in power, expansion, and, later in our history, a remarkable homogeneity are terms that come to mind. A second criteria . . . would be to ask, what is unique in our heritage and in our system? A third criteria is relevance to the present. How did we get here and how can our past explain our present shortcomings and benefits? One further comment on this: when I talk about history, I do not mean current events. Current events are helpful as a starting point in understanding the past, and in arousing interest in the past (the relevance of our present racial dilemma to the passage of Jim Crow laws in the 1890's, for example) . But it is too easy, it would seem, to spend time speculating upon current events—and speculation is all that happens in most high school and college classrooms in this subject—and not spend enough time in noting the historical relationships which are so vital if a student is to understand his society and his own past. A fourth criteria . . . is how can the complexities—or the lack of Utopias in American History—best be taught? A final criteria is to ask how can a teacher deal with as many fields of history as possible, that is, the politics, economics, ideology, cultural history, and international problems? This is to me an important point, for there is nothing easier in American History than to teach political history —and there are few things more irrelevant either. The political chasm which widened and deepened in the 1850's is not understandable in political terms only; one must have some comprehension of the economic, intellectual, ideological, and international problems which faced Pierce, Buchanan, and Lincoln in those years. And while discussing the Civil War, I might add that I am coming more and more to the conclusion that the Civil War is less and less important in American History, even though it is emphasized so strongly in high school and college courses. I suppose there are two reasons for this: one, military history is usually exciting and easy to trace and teach—even though it ranks on the lowest rung of values in the historical hierarchy; second, the fantastic and absurd amount of material which has been ground out since the centennial celebration began in 1961. A social historian, a century from now, is going to do a study of this centennial celebration, and after observing such priceless studies as 'One Hour in the Battle of Gettysburg,' is going to wonder what kind of masochistic society turned out such stuff when there were so many other more important things to investigate and to understand. I hope there are few public schools following the disastrous examples of the professional and popular historians who are intellectually embalmed with the irrelevancies of the Civil War."

Using these suggested criteria as a guide, LaFeber briefly outlined "a chronological approach to American history in which particular periods and events might be emphasized. I am assuming here that this approach is adaptable either for a junior-level narrative survey in which certain periods would be pulled out for closer study, or for a senior-level course which would be concerned more with a problems-approach than with a narrative. I would begin by suggesting that eight eras in American History are most worthy of close attention: (1) The age of discovery—not the voyages themselves, but the European background which spawned the explorers. (2) The development and the decline of Puritan Society in the sixteenth and seventeenth centuries. (3) The shaping of Southern society during the same centuries. (4) The causes of the American Revolution—that is to say the multiplex causes of the Revolution. One of the best ways to approach this, I would suggest, is through Carl Becker's delightful fictional recreation of how one man was torn between British and American allegiances in 1775–1776. Becker realizes the economic, ideological, and power factors as well as the political problems. (5) The Constitutional period. (6) The West in the pre-Civil War period, that is, the growth of Jacksonian democracy, and the causes of the Civil War. (7) The industrial revolution from the Robber Barons to the depression of 1929. (8) The American involvement in the world, 1917–1919, but particularly from 1939 to 1952, with particular emphasis on how a consensus has been reached among most of the American public on the matter of international policy."

LaFeber said that, if asked to choose four of these topics because of limited time, he would list: " (1) Development of Puritan Society and its decline—perhaps the best way to understand the ideological background of most Americans, and certainly a path to the better understanding of political and economic heritage of most Americans. (2) The Constitutional Period—when the assumptions and theories of how a democracy could work on an apparently limitless landed frontier were fought over and finally embodied in a written charter, assumptions and theories which most Americans learned to take so much for granted that with one major exception, they were only infrequently challenged in the next 175 years. (3) The industrial revolution—the basis for modern America. (4) The U.S. involvement in the world between 1917 and 1952 with particular emphasis on the post-World War II period."

As I have pointed out, our three consultants—Donald Kagan, Edward Fox, and Walter LaFeber—were concerned with identifying the topics and ideas that should be taught rather than with relating the concept of structure to their discipline. They objected to the "standard history curriculum" only in so far as it represented a fact-filled, dull, encyclopaedic kind of course. They think history should be alive, and our study group believes that these three historians could make it so. Most of their recommendations pointed the way to a well-taught, thoroughly planned western civilization course in the high school, but a course in no way based upon the concept of structure.

Suggestions for Further Reading

In addition to the items cited in the notes, the reader may wish to consult these references:
Carr, Edward H. *What Is History?* New York: Knopf, 1965.

Dray, William H. *Philosophy of History.* Englewood Cliffs, N.J.: Prentice-Hall, 1964.

Gardiner, Patrick, ed. *Theories of History.* Glencoe, Ill.: Free Press, 1959.

Hughes, H. Stuart. *History as Art and as a Science.* New York: Harper and Row, 1964.

Mazlish, Bruce. *The Riddle of History.* New York: Harper and Row, 1966.

Meyerhoff, Hans, ed. *The Philosophy of History in Our Time.* Garden City, N.Y.: Doubleday, 1959. The writer believes this is the best single book for the nonhistorian on the nature and scope of history.

White, Morton. *Foundations of Historical Knowledge.* New York: Harper and Row, 1965.

[4]

Geography

One of the foremost authorities on geographic education in the United States is Preston James. Professor James of Syracuse University is a distinguished and highly productive scholar in his field—Latin America is his regional specialization—and at the same time he studies, writes, speaks, and consults on the role of geography in the precollege curriculum on almost every occasion at which this topic is seriously considered. He has served on the advisory group for the New York State Education Department in geography and has been a leader in the Project Social Studies activities. In addition, he has written a variety of geography textbooks for a wide range of ages.[1] In acting as a consultant for our study group, James was asked to consider three questions: Does geography have structure? If so, what is your view of it? If not, what geographic content should we teach and how should we decide?

[1] Some of the precollege texts written by James are: Gertrude Whipple and Preston James, *Our Earth* (grades 3 and 4), *Using Our Earth* (grades 3 and 4), *Living on Our Earth* (grades 4 and 5), *At Home on Our Earth* (grades 5 and 6), *Neighbours on Our Earth* (grades 6 and 7), and *Our Earth and Man* (grades 7 and 8), and Preston James and Velda Davis, *Wide World: A Geography* (grades 9 and 10).

A Definition

James's definition for the field was deceptively simple: "Geography has to do with the processes, the sequence of events and all things which make one place on the earth different from any other place." [2] Geography is the study of those characteristics of a place which when combined make it a unique location.

Naturally, all the features of even a fairly small place cannot be studied. For James, one decides which factors to examine on the basis of their total or general significance to the men who live there. "Significance" for this geographer is clearly not to be measured exclusively in physical or economic terms. As he sees it, political, historical, and social as well as physical and economic features that impinge on man in a particular place are a part of the field. James also said that geography is "the development of the principle of spacial integration." It is an inventory of all physical, biotic, and cultural features that occur together "causally" in a particular place or region. It is the scientific study of things and events that may or may not be related in terms of origin or time but which are "causally interconnected" and significant to man in the dimension of space. Elaborating this broad idea in another context, James defined the field by saying that geography "deals with the associations of phenomena that give special character to particular places and with the likenesses and differences among places." [3]

Before we examine the James position further, it seems wise to present a few additional definitions. They are basic-

[2] Speech at Cornell, Jan. 15, 1964.

[3] Preston James and Clarence Jones, eds., *American Geography: Inventory and Prospect* (Syracuse, N.Y.: Syracuse University Press, 1954).

ally consistent with James's, and they seem helpful in developing a better understanding of his briefly stated notion. Richard Hartshorne's excellent monograph *Perspective on the Nature of Geography*—probably the best short treatment of methodological questions available in the field of geography—presents a number of definitions that Hartshorne believes are particularly useful. One of those which he regards to be of greatest importance is that of the highly influential German geographer, Alfred Hettner. Hettner determined the basic pattern for modern accounts of the nature of geography with his 1927 statement:

The goal of the chorological [geographical] point of view is to know the character of regions and places through comprehension of the existence together and interrelation among the different realms of reality and their varied manifestations, and to comprehend the earth surface as a whole in its actual arrangement in continents, larger and smaller regions and places.[4]

Another definition by Vidal de la Blache, perhaps France's most distinguished geographer, is paraphrased by Hartshorne as follows:

Geography is the science of places, concerned with the qualities and potentialities of countries. The particular character of a country is expressed by the totality of its features, the social diversities associated with the diversities of places.[5]

Hartshorne also likes the *American College Dictionary* definition, which describes the field as:

[4] Hartshorne, *Perspective on the Nature of Geography* (Chicago: Rand McNally, 1959), p. 13.
[5] *Ibid.*, p. 14.

Structure and the Social Studies

The study of the areal differentiation of the earth surface, as shown in the character, arrangement, and interrelations over the earth of elements such as climate, relief, soil, vegetation, population, land use, industries or states and of the unit areas formed by the complex of these individual elements.

All three of these definitions give the reader a clearer idea of what James meant by "associations of phenomena," "special character" of places, and "likenesses and differences among places."

James amplified his definition by discussing the history and development of geography as a distinct field of study. His ideas on this subject can be found in his chapter in *Social Studies and the Social Sciences*,[6] so we will not restate them here; but it does seem essential to indicate that James believes that the organization scheme provided by Immanuel Kant gives the appropriate classification system of knowledge necessary for understanding the nature and function of geography. Parenthetically, James is aware of the contemporary criticisms of Kant's plan, but apparently is not convinced by the arguments.[7]

In Kant's tripartite system, knowledge is organizable into three and only three classes: substantive or systematic, chronological, and chorological. The substantive category groups together for study purposes topics of like or similar origin. Sociology, anthropology, economics, and government are examples from the social sciences of disciplines organized in this way. In these cases the study of groups, cultures, resource allocations, and power, respectively, are the

[6] New York: Harcourt, Brace and World, 1962.
[7] For a brief but helpful description of these criticisms see Jan O. M. Broek, *Geography: Its Scope and Spirit* (Columbus, Ohio: Merrill, 1965), p. 14.

substantive topics which provide, at the same time, the subject matter and the plan of organization for these disciplines. The chronological areas of knowledge are those that are concerned with bits and pieces of information and broader ideas and generalizations that are organized together because they are associated in time—they occurred at the same period, moment, era, or epoch. The study of modes of transportation, speech styles, letters, art objects, ways of making a living, the prevailing form of government, and so on—the totality of the way of life of men at a particular time and the comparison of these diverse elements at different periods of time is the legitimate domain of chronological studies. For our purposes, history is the obvious example. Kant's system does not intend to eliminate considerations of time or history in substantive fields, but only to define the emphasis and focus. In this classification plan, one might trace the historical development of a particular use and arrangement of power—this would be political science; one might also study the totality of life, including the prevailing form of government during a specific time—this is history. (As we have seen, many modern historians would be unhappy with this dichotomy.) Kant's final category— chorological—is concerned with things grouped together because they are associated in space. Astronomy is such a field, but for us, geography is the prototype. James's acceptance of the Kant scheme and his definition place geography in a unique category in this book. The social sciences, history, and geography are three distinct types or areas of scholarship with categorically different ways of organizing knowledge.

In summary, geography is concerned with all things relevant to an understanding of man that are associated with a particular place.

Structure and the Social Studies

Methodological and Organizational Questions

So much for definition, but closely related problems remain. Before we turn to the specific content that our consultant and others have recommended, there are some important methodological and organizational questions to be considered. Hopefully, these issues will be accurately identified here, but we will make no real attempt to resolve them. These are problems that have traditionally and continually plagued the field. They have no simple answers. Still, one needs to understand what these problems are in order to comprehend the issues involved in the process of selecting the content for geographic study.

The first is the problem of the tremendous scope of the field of geography or, perhaps better put, the heterogeneity of the geographer's interests. There is a common charge that geography is a study of everything and, consequently, a scientific investigation of nothing.

As far as I was able to learn from Professor James or from any other geographer, the only "answer" to this assertion is to admit the breadth of interest, but to argue that there are two limits to the scope that do provide an adequate basis for selectivity. These limits are the focus on a specific place and only that place and the inclusion of factors for study associated with that place only if they have relevance and significance for understanding the men who live there. Many geographers go further and claim that their problem in this regard is precisely like the one faced by historians—no more or less difficult—the only difference is that time has been replaced by space. Hartshorne, however, seems to believe that geography has greater breadth than history:

In the space sciences other than geography, the phenomena . . . are limited to inanimate nature. In history, as limited to the period of literate history, natural phenomena have been relatively constant, so that in the integrations which history studies, the variable factors are largely limited to human elements. But the earth's surface is unique to our geographic knowledge as an object which consists of integrations formed by a great diversity of inanimate, biological and social phenomena, varying in significant interrelations from place to place. The goal of geography, the comprehension of the earth's surface, involves therefore the analysis and synthesis of integrations composed of interrelated phenomena of the greatest degree of heterogeneity of perhaps any field of science.[8]

Where does this leave us? Where we started—geography has tremendous scope and geographers face the selectivity problem constantly and consistently. The "limits" just cited are wide indeed. In terms of curriculum the question is: Is the scope so great and so loose that geography does not provide a meaningful framework? For what it is worth, every member of our study group believed that geography offered a very useful organization scheme at least in terms of the elementary and secondary school curriculum.

A second basic issue is the sticky dualism of considering geography to be either a social science or a physical science. We read and hear such terms as "human geography," "physical geography," "cultural geography," and "place geography." These designations suggest a dichotomy, a black-and-white distinction, between human and non-human aspects of the field. Drawing this distinction has become known in the field as "environmentalism." It assumes that understanding man must begin with a separate study of his physical environment and lead to a study of his social milieu.

James believes that such dualistic thinking is detrimental to the field and that it represents a basic misunderstanding

8 *Perspective,* p. 35.

of the nature of geography. He argues that geography can and must be subdivided for purposes of specialized study, but that the human-nonhuman distinction does not provide a proper basis for classification. Furthermore, he believes that while this division has historically made some sense in other disciplines, it has become less and less tenable everywhere. He points out that the traditional lines of separation between physics, chemistry, biology, mathematics, the social sciences, and other fields are in a state of rapid change. Biophysics, mathematical sociology, biochemistry, econometrics are recognized now as legitimate fields, or at least areas, of study. In addition, James argues that geography is neither a social nor a physical science in the usual meaning, for it is a bridging field, if indeed any gap for which a bridge is needed does exist. It is a uniting field. It draws on the social sciences and on the natural sciences and, in fact, on every other division of human knowledge. It must be emphasized, however, that geography is not organized on the same basis as the systematic or substantive sciences. It cannot be grouped in terms of our traditional pattern—the physical sciences, the biological sciences, the social sciences, the humanities, and the arts. It borrows from and contributes to all of these. Unlike history, however, geography's methodology, goals, and organization seem to make it primarily a branch of science.

Although James objects to this dualism in geography and emphasizes the discipline's inclusive nature, it must also be said that the National Council for the Social Studies yearbook on geography which he edited in 1959 included these two chapters: "Professional Contributions to Physical Geography" and "Progress in Human Geography." [9] So al-

[9] *New Viewpoints in Geography* (Washington, D.C.: National Education Association, 1959).

though dualism may be an incorrect way to regard the field, it certainly is prevalent even among those professional geographers who deny its validity.

Even if we assume that geography is neither a social nor a physical science, we still run into problems. For example, should geography be administratively grouped with the social sciences or the physical sciences or neither? In an educational institution, the budget, housing, curriculum, staffing, and other matters would be directly tied to this decision. Perhaps of greater importance, should geography teachers be armed with a strong minor concentration in one of the physical sciences—geology, chemistry, physics, astronomy—or in a social science? Does it matter? Some have argued that students in geography should be prepared in both the physical and the social sciences. Is this possible or will the student be spread too thin? Are the appropriate research methods and procedures those of the social scientist or of the physical scientist or of neither or of both? In short, where does the subject belong in the curriculum and organization of the secondary school?

Undoubtedly, our answer to this last question is apparent, since geography is included in this book. With our orientation, geography is a study of social man first and foremost, and, therefore, the focus is on the social sciences. Given the academic organization that exists, it is not possible to treat geography all by itself. It must be grouped somewhere, and we think it belongs in the social studies curriculum. Probably an equally strong case could be made for the opposite arrangement, but not if one views geography as James does.

An extension of this physical-social question is the problem of how geography should be subdivided. As has already been indicated, for scholarly purposes the field must be broken down into manageable parts. A man simply cannot be an expert—a researcher—in all of geography at once. If the professors of geography reject the human-nonhuman dichotomy, then what division scheme do they accept?

Hartshorne states the problem succinctly in his ninth chapter heading, "Is Geography Divided between 'Systematic' and 'Regional' Geography?" [10] He asks whether it is appropriate for a specific geographer, for example, to be a student of river valley cultures across the dimensions of space and time; or should the specialist concentrate on a particular place; or are both these specializations appropriate ways of working in geography? Clearly, the nature of research and field work would differ in these two approaches.

Before we consider this question, another must be raised. This different but closely associated issue might be expressed with the question: Is the ultimate goal of geography to study and understand and explain man's interaction with the earth's surface in *general*—to perceive broadly his relations to climate, land use patterns, or culture groups, for instance; or is the primary objective to know a specific area in all its many details? Are we looking for general geographic laws and principles and description or depth studies of special places? Is an understanding of "general geography" or of "special geography" the basic goal we seek? One might also ask whether systematic (or general) study is in fact appropriately labeled geography or is it a substantive science, in Kant's terms? To restate the two-pronged question: Is geography a "special" study divided either by regions or topics, or is it a "general," world-wide, all-topics study?

James insists that geography is inevitably and desirably all of these. In fact he lists twenty-four subdivisions of the field

[10] *Perspective,* p. 108.

and thinks research should continue in all of them.[11] He perceives no serious problems resulting from having different geographers or even the same man look at the field in a variety of ways at various times. However, all geographers must be aware of the other approaches and try to be aware of research in the broad field. In fact, it is necessary for geographers to view the subject in its totality as a combination of these divisions and approaches.

In sum, geography cannot be considered as divided between studies which analyze individual elements over the world and those which analyze complete complexes of elements by areas. The former are logically a part of the appropriate systematic sciences, the latter simply cannot be carried out. All studies in geography analyze the areal variations and connections of phenomena in integration. There is no dichotomy or dualism, but rather a gradational range along a continuum from those which analyze the most elementary complexes in areal variation over the world to those which analyze the most complex integrations in areal variation within small areas. The former we may appropriately call "topical" studies, the latter "regional" studies, provided we remember that every truly geographic study involves the use of both the topical and the regional approach.[12]

So, then, it is appropriate at times to subdivide geography in terms of regions. Sometimes this is done by using cultural types (James, as we shall see, promotes this division criterion); other times the regions are divided on the basis of physical or biotic features. Although these criteria are the most common, it is possible to divide the world into many other types of regions. It is also appropriate to divide geog-

11 James and Jones, *American Geography,* pp. x–xi.
12 Hartshorne, *Perspective,* pp. 121–122.

raphy in terms of topics of interest such as geomorphology and climatology. Other areas such as cartography or even demography have at times been considered to be specializations within geography. In sum, the field does not seem to have a tight logical system for dividing itself.

The next problem to be mentioned may spring from or lead to the previous question. At any rate, they are related. The issue can be stated in a word—determinism. Environmentalism, which was discussed earlier, almost inevitably leads the unsophisticated to the notion that if we are given physical features A, B, and C, man will develop in a predictable way. That is, physical and biotic conditions determine the culture. But, as we know, modern geographers including James go to great lengths to deny determinism and even "possibilism." In his remarks at Cornell, James cited many examples in an effort to show that man's knowledge, attitudes, and skills at any given time and place are more important to his development than are his physical, climatic, and biotic resources. In fact, the very idea of "natural resources" is unacceptable to James. One man's resources are another man's hindrances. Most so-called resources are valuable only because of the culture. For example, the importance of climate is entirely relative. The Chilean desert is ideal for mining copper, but hopeless in terms of agriculture. A mountain range may be a serious detriment to the development of one society, while the same range at another time or even at the same time a few miles to the north may be literally worshipped as the most significant feature in protecting and/or advancing human life. James argues that a modern nation such as Japan has made a bare-faced lie out of geographic determinism. In this case, so-called geographic laws have been resoundingly disproved. Still, determinism or possibilism is *the* lesson a large number of geography texts would have us learn. And, according to James, a good many geography teachers promote determinism.

It is not easy to strike out determinism in our thinking, and if we do, there is a serious problem with what is left. James himself wants students "to seek geographic causes." Can one seek and presumably find geographic causes without being partially a determinist? The answer is probably Yes, but the question poses difficulties, to say the least. Classroom exercises in which students are given partially complete maps or sets of geographic conditions and are then asked to describe what life would be like there are frequently proposed by geographers. Students are asked to tell where the cities would be or give the likely locations for commercial agriculture or trade routes. Is this determinism? Where does one draw the line between determinism, possibilism, probabalism, and sound, scholarly geographic induction? This matter continues to be a concern, and it should be reflected in the thinking and planning of geography teachers at all levels.

A final problem that should be mentioned is concerned with a phase of the inquiry and reporting procedures of geographers which is practically unique to them. To be sure, most of the methods of geography are common to other disciplines; much of the discussion of methodology in the next chapter is pertinent. However, geography has a particular need to perceive areal realtionships and as a consequence has developed a special tool, the map. Students of geography even at elementary levels must understand maps:

In the process of finding out what the earth is like, geographers have had to face the problem of how to communicate knowledge about the earth. There is one great difference between the writing of history and the writing of geography. Words are organized in sentences, paragraphs, chapters—always to be read in sequence. The sequence of events in history is reproduced in words that follow one another through the same time dimension. But geography deals with things that are located beside each other, at the same moment of time. Word descriptions that must be read in sequence provide a poor vehicle for reproducing areal relations. The language of the map is ideal for such a purpose.[13]

James goes on to say that people have to be taught to read maps. They do not do it naturally. Teachers take for granted that pupils understand the scale of maps and the use of symbols, but they are wrong in so doing. He argues that geographic instruction at all levels must raise regularly such basic questions as: What are the purposes of maps? What types are available? What are their shortcomings? How well do they do the job for which they were intended? What are the advantages and disadvantages of various types? How about globes—how can they be used most effectively? What is the relationship between map projections and the function of the map? What is the relation among different types of distortions, for example, size, shape, direction, and distance? How can the map maker use propaganda techniques? To be sure, the answers to some of these questions are difficult, indeed not fully known, but it is vital to raise the issues in a study of geography.

Hopefully, the major methodological and organizational questions of geography have been identified. It should be remembered that these process matters are a definite part of the structure of the field. Students studying geography even at the elementary level must be concerned with these issues.

[13] James, *Social Studies and Social Sciences,* p. 58.

Place of Geography in the Curriculum

As would be expected, in spite of these problems Professor James believes that geography provides a unique and essential opportunity for study in the social studies curriculum for elementary and secondary schools. His notion of the specific role of geography in the curriculum seems consistent with his ideas regarding the organizational and methodological questions just identified and with his acceptance of Kant's classification system.

James wants all public school pupils, bright and dull, to think and study geographically or chorologically in the elementary school and again in the secondary school. Further, he thinks almost all the directors of the national curriculum projects in the social sciences and history agree with him and accept the notion that the total social studies program ought to include some chronological social study (history) some substantive social study (anthropology, sociology, government, economics) and some chorological social study (geography). In fact, James said that "he has not found any people from any of the disciplines related to the social studies curriculum who would exclude any one of the three broad areas." [14] To be sure, he admits, as we saw in Chapter 1, that there are sharp differences of opinion regarding the emphasis which should be given to the various areas.

James was willing to give his "best guess" regarding the most appropriate levels for systematic, time, and space studies. He did so with much hesitance, pointing out that solid information on which to base such a decision was lacking. On "logical and intuitive" grounds, however, he would like substantive organization to be used from kindergarten

[14] Speech at Cornell, Jan. 15, 1964.

through the third grade. The focus would be anthropological, sociological, and psychological. The children would study human behavior in terms of cultures, groups, and individuals.[15] Then geography should be introduced. Chorological principles, ideas, and concepts should be used as the content core and the basis for organization in grades four, five, and six. The curriculum of these intermediate grades should be centered on regional studies. The specific regions should be determined primarily be distinctive physical or biotic characteristics—what James calls natural regions. (Later in this chapter more of his specific ideas on the intermediate grade program are given.) James suggests an introduction to the chronological approach in grades seven and eight with an elementary study of the nature of history and a survey of the historical development of the local and national communities. In grades nine and ten James would return to the chorological approach. This time, cultural regions would be studied. He believes that the present state of scholarship points to eleven such regions.[16] History and the substantive social sciences would not be ignored during the ninth and tenth grades, but the focus would be geographical. In grades eleven and twelve

[15] James pointed out that his basic ideas are utilized in the primary school curriculum developed by Educational Services Incorporated (now the Educational Development Center). However, he criticized certain specific aspects of the E.S.I. program. For example, he questions the use of the baboon and the Eskimo as subjects for case studies; while he believes that depth studies are appropriate, he feels that they should be completed with important cultures as models. The Social Studies Curriculum Project of E.S.I. is mentioned in Chapter 1 (page 18), and Douglas L. Oliver discusses the organization in Chapter 6.

[16] For a complete and fascinating discussion of James's culture region approach see his *One World Divided* (New York: Blaisdell, 1964).

James would return to the substantive approach with a study of current social, political, and economic world problems. Thus James would use geography as the organizing discipline in five of the thirteen years of the social studies program—a greater emphasis on the subject than it typically receives. It also means that history would be de-emphasized to a considerable degree.

Structure

James believes in the idea of structure as we have defined it. For teaching purposes he divides the content of geography into three main categories, and he places the methodology that should be taught into a fourth. These four subdivisions contain his structure of the field.

The first category, which he calls simply habitat, is the non-man-made parts of the environment. James describes habitat as the natural environment. He makes a distinction between culture and habitat on the basis of the division between man-made versus natural phenomenon. All aspects of the environment may be placed in one or the other of these categories. To be certain, at many points the two overlap. For example, a plowed, fertilized, drained, alkalized field is both a product of the culture and of the habitat.

Habitat includes minerals, plants, and animals. It may be divided into four spheres. There is the atmosphere, composed of gases that immediately surround the earth. The state of the atmosphere at a given time and place is, of course, our weather and is of tremendous import to the geographer. Then there is the lithosphere, the rock crust of the earth including the soil. The hydrosphere includes the oceans, seas, rivers and streams, lakes, ground water, glaciers, and ice caps. The biosphere contains the plants and animals which are living in a natural state partially as a result of conditions in the other three spheres. Children should understand the meaning of habitat, atmosphere, lithosphere, hydrosphere, and biosphere at an early age. The relationship between the spheres and their impact on man should be explored in as much depth as possible in grades four, five, and six and even before.

James believes the best way to study habitat is to examine the surface of the earth in terms of natural regions. He suggests nine such regions: (1) high latitude and high altitude —tundra and permanent snow lands; (2) higher middle latitudes of the Northern Hemisphere, west coasts north of 60 degrees, east coasts north of 45 degrees, and lands extending across the continental interiors—evergreen or needle-leaf forests; (3) east sides of continents between 25 degrees and 45 degrees and west sides of continents between 40 degrees and 60 degrees—midlatitude mixed forests; (4) west coasts of continents between 30 degrees and 40 degrees— Mediterranean scrub woodlands; (5) dry margin of midlatitude forests—prairies; (6) transition areas between humid forest lands and dry lands—steppes; (7) west coasts of continents between 20 degrees and 30 degrees and continental interiors in the middle latitudes—deserts; (8) low latitudes and lower middle latitudes on margins of dry lands and transitional areas between humid forests and deserts— tropical woodlands and savanna; (9) east coasts of continents for about 25 degrees on either side of the equator, west coasts for 10 degrees on either side of the equator, equatorial lowlands, and rainy islands—tropical forests.

The concepts used here to describe the regions—latitude, longitude, altitude, for instance—should be understood by all pupils. They need to know what the regions are like geographically—not just the physical features. In studying the natural regions the traditional myths and half-truths that have persistently plagued the teaching of geography for many years must be assiduously avoided. For example, one should not teach a course in geography based on the division of the earth into continents. These categories of land mass are almost totally insignificant in terms of geographic principles and generalizations. One cannot make many meaningful statements about Africa as a whole; this land is too diverse and broad. One can, however, make some useful generalizations about the equatorial lowlands. Similarly, the Aristotelian myth of temperate, torrid, and frigid zones must not be promulgated. Although geographers have been saying this for many years, the idea is still being taught. Teachers still believe and teach that "torrid" lands are hotter than "temperate" lands, even though it is not so. Children ought to be taught, however, that climates in the world are developed symmetrically on the land masses. They need to know that if a geographer knows the latitude of a place, its altitude, its location in relation to mountains, and whether it is located on the eastern, western, or central portions of a continent, he then knows a great deal about the climate.

The pupil should be taught the nature and relationship of the four "spheres" of habitat. In his study of the atmosphere, he should learn to understand its composition, the nature of the wind cycle, and the elements of measuring and recording climatic changes. The "why" of his weather should be emphasized. The relationship between meteorology, climatology, and geography should be explored.

The study of the lithosphere should emphasize the dynamic nature of the crust of the earth and the significance of geomorphic change for man. Erosion is a central idea. The fascinating workings of water, wind, and ice should be explained with ever-increasing sophistication. The various processes used by the scientist to obtain knowledge about the earth's surface should also be explored in as much depth as possible.

James emphasized that surface features of the earth are not symmetrically arranged. They are unique. Teachers need to take their pupils as far as possible in learning the important land forms, though not by rote or meaningless associations. Every educated man should know, for example, where the Andes are and, at least in part, what their significance to man has been.

The hydrosphere also demands attention. The nature, potential power, and supply of water should be explored. James believes the secrets of the sea should be as interesting to pupils as the secrets of outer space. The hydrographic cycle should be emphasized. The ways in which the water resources specialist and oceanographer work are also important.

The study of plants and animals (the biosphere) should focus on the belts of natural vegetation cover and associated animal life, and how man has been affected by them, and how he has used and changed them.

This aspect of teaching habitat is related to James's second major category—the relations between man and the land. This topic seems to follow naturally from the study of habitat; in fact, the division seems artificial. The reason for setting the idea apart as a separate category is to emphasize its importance:

The significance to man of his physical and biotic habitat is a function of his attitudes, objectives, and technical skills. That is, culture determines the significance and meaning of habitat. . . . The meaning of habitat changes with any significant shift in the culture.[17]

17 James's speech at Cornell, Jan. 15, 1964.

James gave many, many examples—cotton needs a 200-day growing season, 20-inch rainfall is necessary for grain crops, hilly uplands lead to dairy farming, coal is necessary for heavy industry—of so-called geographic laws which are, in fact, utterly false. In other words, the most significant lesson to be learned here is antideterminism.

Another idea that James would have emphasized is the notion of the land hemisphere. If we cut the globe in half so that Nantes, France, is at the center of one hemisphere, we will include most of the land mass of the world. The other hemisphere will contain mostly water, plus Antarctica, Australia, part of Indonesia, and New Zealand, smaller islands of the Pacific, and the southern end of South America. The land hemisphere contains 90 per cent of the inhabited land, 94 per cent of the people, and 98 per cent of the world's economic production.

James believes this division of the world, which gives the central position to western Europe, is a useful way of looking at and studying the world. He argues that such a division is significantly related to communication, transportation, commerce, and world power. (Parenthetically, the idea fails to excite this writer, and I wonder if it deserves the attention James has given it.)

The third and final content category is centered around the concept of cultural region. James divides the world into eleven such regions: European, Soviet, Anglo-American, Latin American, North African–Southwest Asian, South Asian, Southeast Asian, East Asian, African, Australian–New Zealand, and Pacific. He claims that students should study the world geographically using these divisions after they have been exposed to the natural regions. The reasoning here seems quite straightforward. If culture determines the significance of habitat, then a study of geography ought to be focused on culture at least at some time in the education of man. James thinks that organization by cultural region ought to follow organization by natural region because cultural regionism is a more sophisticated idea. He would have us focus on both the unique features of cultures and the similarities between them. The child would be led to ask why cultures have distinctive characteristics.

In addition to the background gained by habitat and land-man relationship studies, James would introduce the specific study of the various culture regions with a depth study of the meaning of the concepts of race and culture. He borrows from anthropology here for his definitions, and he particularly likes the Herskovits' description of culture, with its five categories of cultural phenomena: material culture—tools and technical skills, economic systems; social institutions—social organization, education, political groups, government; attitude toward the unknown—religious beliefs, magic; art—graphic and plastic arts, folklore; and language.[18]

In addition, James would emphasize briefly as background what he calls "historical geography." The important ideas, he suggests, center on the belief that human history has been characterized both by long periods in which relatively little cultural change took place and by revolutionary times when dramatic cultural changes occurred. For James there are three periods of cultural revolution. The first was the Agricultural Revolution, starting approximately 8,000 B.C. The second, starting about 4,000 B.C., was the Rise of Early Civilizations, and the third involved the twin movements of the Industrial Revolution and the Democratic Revolution. We are now in the midst of this latest period of change, which began approximately two hundred years ago.

[18] James, *One World Divided,* p. 14.

There is not time to develop this idea here. James has discussed the idea fully in a number of places, including his junior high school text *The Wide World*. Briefly, James wants the nature of these revolutions studied in terms of the ways in which they have affected our contemporary culture. For James, the adaptations to these developments have led to the cultural differences that make cultural regions distinct. Such a study would help us understand the causes of and consequences of our present cultural divisions.

Of major importance in this area is the matter of human population. Students should examine carefully current and past census data. They should be asked to try to explain them and project from them. Distribution, movement, density, and growth of population within and between cultural regions must receive considerable attention.

James, of course, cautions against oversimplifications and adds these warnings: (1) No cultural region is completely uniform. There are numerous exceptions within each of them. (2) "Region" is not an exact or precise concept in terms of physical boundaries. (3) Each region has a prototype cultural core, but the peripheries are transitional, borrowing from two or more cores. The core is not necessarily in the middle of the region in terms of distance. (4) The cultural regions that exist today are shifting and have changed constantly. The rate of change itself varies. Habitat changes too. In fact, change is the very center of the historical-geographical approach. Historical geography is a study of change.

The final category in the structure of geography is concerned with methods of inquiry. As we know, there is an emphasis on map skills and on the development of a sense or an awareness of space and spatial relationships. Much has been written on this topic, and there seems little point in developing it here.[19] But, to repeat, James believes strongly that pupils graduating from our high schools must be able to read maps with understanding. This skill is as necessary to geographic literacy as being able to read the printed page. Finally, children should study the process matters mentioned earlier in this chapter under Methodological and Organization Questions.

Summary

James has written his own summary of what the study of geography can contribute to the education of students and what the educated student should know:

1. Our one world is differentiated by variations in the physical and biotic character of habitats, and by variations in the resource base of states [natural regions].

2. It is differentiated, also, by variations in the population, the economy, and the political conditions.

[because]

3. For some two centuries two great processes of fundamental and revolutionary change—the Industrial Revolution and the Democratic Revolution—have been going on, and have been spreading unevenly from the culture hearth around the North Sea.

4. As the two revolutions spread they also undergo a continuation of the process of development, so that they do not make the same impact today along their advancing fronts as they did a century ago.

5. Distinctive social, economic, and political reactions have been produced by the impact of these revolutionary changes on

[19] One particularly useful presentation is the brief chapter by Lorrin Kennamer entitled "Developing a Sense of Time and Place," in Helen Carpenter, ed., *Skill Development in the Social Studies* (Washington, D.C.: National Education Association, 1963).

pre-existing societies—the pre-industrial and pre-democratic societies.

6. In each distinctive culture area, so defined, the significance to man of the features of the habitat changes with changes in the culture, requiring with each change a new evaluation of the resource base.

7. Such re-evaluation is aided by grouping the resulting cultures into culture regions, in each of which there is a distinctive association of demographic conditions, economic development, and political expression.

8. This distinctive regional character is most clearly observable in the cores of the regions.

9. Eleven such regions can tentatively be defined; this number may be subject to change as a result of more precise study or the continuation of the revolutionary processes.

10. The geographic arrangement of these distinctive regions on the globe has a meaning not found in the separate consideration of the elements that make them up, and this meaning is relevant to the formulation of economic, political, or military policy.[20]

These ten understandings plus map and space skills are, to James, the structure of geography.

We might close with a very concise statement on what geography is all about—one which seems to sum up what James has said:

The geographer must learn about the biophysical features of the earth; is deeply interested in the interrelations between society and habitat; needs to read the cultural landscape as the earth-engraved expression of man's activity; inspects and compares distributional patterns; and formulates concepts and principles. All these means, each part of the whole, together serve the purpose of geography: to understand the earth as the

[20] *One World Divided,* p. 421.

world of man, with particular reference to the differentiation and integration of places.[21]

Suggestions for Further Reading

In addition to the items cited in the notes, the reader may wish to consult these references:

Freeman, T. W. *A Hundred Years of Geography*. Chicago: Aldine, 1962.

Hanna, Paul R., and others. *Geography in the Teaching of Social Studies*. New York: Houghton Mifflin, 1966.

High School Geography Project. Newsletter and a variety of bulletins. Association of American Geographers, 1146 Sixteenth Street, N.W., Washington, D.C. 20036.

Hill, Wilhelmina, ed. *Curriculum Guide for Geographic Education*. Normal, Ill.: National Council for Geographic Education, 1964.

Journal of Geography. Monthly on the teaching of geography; Normal, Ill.: National Council for Geographic Education.

Kohn, Clyde F. "Geography," in *Teaching the New Social Studies in Secondary Schools: An Inductive Approach*. Ed. Edwin Fenton. New York: Holt, Rinehart and Winston, 1966.

Kolezon, Edward R. and Rubin Maloff. *Vitalizing Geography in the Classroom*. New York: Teachers Practical Press, 1964.

Stimson, Lillian W. "Geography," in *The Social Sciences Foundations of the Social Studies*. Ed. John U. Michaelis and A. M. Johnston. Boston: Allyn and Bacon, 1965.

Teaching About World Regions. Albany, N.Y.: New York State Education Department, 1963.

Wagner, P. L., and M. W. Mikesell, eds., *Readings in Cultural Geography*. Chicago: University of Chicago Press, 1962.

[21] Broek, *Geography*, p. 79.

[5]

Sociology

The field of sociology was represented at the colloquium by Robin Williams of Cornell University. In addition to being a highly respected sociologist, Professor Williams has been a member since its inception of the executive committee of the high school curriculum project of the American Sociological Association (A.S.A.).[1] This group is developing units, called episodes, on sociological topics for the secondary schools. It is also producing a series of paperbacks and a full-year sociology course. In his description of the A.S.A. project, Williams noted that the staff has at least partially accepted the idea of structure. That is, their activities are centered on a study of the foundational principles and basic methods of inquiry of sociology which should be taught to all youngsters.

Nature of Sociology

Williams said at the outset that he did not want to give a formal definition of sociology. He believes that it is difficult to produce truly satisfactory definitions for any of the social

[1] "Sociological Resources for Secondary Schools," a curriculum project of the American Sociological Association, University of Michigan, Ann Arbor, Michigan.

sciences, primarily because human behavior cannot be categorized into tight, neat compartments, and this fact inevitably results in an overlap in the interests of the various fields of study. He did make a series of statements, however, which provide at least a partial definition. When we add this description to the specific content he recommended, we have, as he put it, placed "a circle around sociology," even if we do not have a precise analytic definition.

"Sociology," Williams said, "is the scientific study of group processes and structures [organization patterns] and the social and cultural causes and consequences of those processes and structures." [2] The basic idea on which sociology is based is that individual behavior is profoundly influenced by relationships with groups. Attempts to understand how and why and when and where these group associations affect our behavior is the substance of sociology.

"Sociology is really the study of status and role," Williams went on to say. "If we can teach a pupil to analyze a community, a family, a church, a classroom or any human group in terms of what is expected of its members; then we are teaching sociology and at the same time giving the pupils a very helpful way of looking at life." Sociologists are interested in studying the rules, norms, roles, statuses, and ways of behaving in groups which already exist, and in the process of forming new or reorganized groups of all types and sizes. The process of inducting group members is also a vital concern—in fact, the whole area provided by the individual's reaction to his changing group associations is of fundamental significance to the sociologist.

If I have the general notion of a social position, a status, and understand that people who occupy different social positions

2 Speech at Cornell, Nov. 25, 1965.

are expected to play different roles; and if I know that every role we play articulates with other roles—if I begin to see society as a seamless web of these positions, endlessly, throughout the whole social system; and if I then see that in each case there are the conformity processes at work here—people bringing expectations and demands to bear on individuals who occupy social positions and rewarding or punishing them by the way they react to their performance; if I see all this—these simple concepts—I have a basic understanding of sociology and a useful way of dealing with my world. I can go into any group, any situation, any community, and ask myself a set of questions. I can say, what is the organization? What is expected of me? What does that office or title mean? What are its rights and obligations? What do people expect of it? How do we share the task and how do we find out who does what? [3]

This according to Williams is sociology. Most of his terms will be described more specifically later, but first let us turn to the organization of the field.

Organization

The field of sociology has been organized in a variety of ways by a variety of scholars. Williams' plan of organization will be offered here to provide further insight into his views regarding the structure of the field. He believes that the major topics are: work and occupations; family; education; mobility; public opinion; communications; political sociology; community organization; collective behavior in "high voltage areas," such as crazes, fads, mobs, and riots; crime, including delinquency; health and medicine ("hospital sociology") ; small groups; personality and group processes; social change; research methodology; and sociology of the arts. These are the areas of greatest concern to the sociolo-

[3] *Ibid.*

gist, but Williams was emphatic in his contention that none of these is the exclusive domain of sociology.

Before turning to Williams' specific structural suggestions, we should examine the ideas of a few other sociologists on the nature and organization of the field. These schema are provided in order to amplify Williams' ideas and not to argue with him. They are more detailed, because they were prepared for different purposes.

Caroline Rose presents an organization pattern which is in some ways distinctly different from the Williams plan, but not contradictory.[4] Its simplicity is attractive. She divides sociology into five areas:

1. Social organization or social structure. This area is primarily interested in "classifying and analyzing the structure of groups and in studying the relations among them."[5]

2. Social psychology. Here one is mainly interested in collective behavior, the relationships between the group and its members, and in socialization—the process of becoming human.

3. History of sociology and the sociology of knowledge. This specialization is interested in how the discipline developed and why it evolved in the way it has. It includes the philosophical branch of sociology, so it might be considered to be the humanities division of the field.

4. Social problems. Sociologists in this category are concerned with the nature and solution of social issues which are currently troublesome. Some examples of contemporary importance are criminology, medical sociology, immigration, minority group relations, industrial sociology, and

---

[4] Caroline B. Rose, *Sociology: The Study of Man in Society* (Columbus, Ohio: Merrill, 1965), ch. 1.

[5] *Ibid.*, p. 4.

educational sociology. The social problems area is perceived to have a distinctly different focus from the other subdivisions. For one thing, the topics shift with time. An area will be emphasized for a period and then be almost totally ignored. "New" areas are continually being introduced. Medical sociology, for example, has suddenly received a great deal of attention. Also, this category usually does not provide an arena for "pure" or basic research. It is applied sociology; and it is almost always interdisciplinary. The study of social problems leads one almost inevitably to other subject matter. One cannot adequately study criminology without some understanding of economics, politics, and other fields.

5. Demography or population studies. Actually, Rose believes that this area is a separate discipline, closely allied with sociology, but distinct. She includes it in her listing apparently only because of its proximity to sociological studies. The reader will recall that geography also claimed very close connections with this field.

A still different system is presented in the very readable little book by Alex Inkeles entitled *What Is Sociology?* [6] He structures the discipline according to four areas:

1. Sociological analysis. This area includes the study of human culture and society, sociological perspective, and the scientific method in social science.

2. Primary units of social life. Here the sociologist is interested in social acts and social relationships, the individual personality, groups (including ethnic and class), communities—urban and rural, associations and organizations, populations, and society.

3. Basic social institutions. This area is concerned with

[6] *What is Sociology? An Introduction to the Discipline and Profession* (Englewood Cliffs, N.J.: Prentice-Hall, 1966), p. 12.

the family and kinship and with economic, political and legal, religious, educational and scientific, recreational and welfare, and aesthetic and expressive institutions.

4. Fundamental social processes. The processes studied by the sociologist in this area include differentiation and stratification, cooperation, accommodation, and assimilation, social conflict (including revolution and war), communication (including opinion formation, expression, and change), socialization and indoctrination, social evaluation (the study of values), social control, social deviance (crime, suicide, etc.), social integration, and social change.

The Inkeles organization has the greatest appeal of any I have seen, but, again, I see no contradiction between it and the Williams plan.

One possible outcome—perhaps the most likely outcome —of examining these three organizational patterns, is an awareness of the tremendous scope of the field of sociology. It should be perfectly clear that these topics are of concern to other disciplines; they are not the exclusive property of sociology. Still, simply because sociologists will admit to an interest in this sweeping range of topics, the enormous breadth of the field is dramatically apparent.

Methods

But sociology is more than a list of topics or an organization plan. Inkeles says:

To understand sociology we obviously need to know something about the subject matter. But even more fundamental in defining the character of any discipline are the questions it asks about its subject matter and the ways in which it goes about answering them. Lists of subjects, such as have been presented, tell us what sociology deals with without quite answering the question: "What is sociology all about?" We are, so far, in the position of a student who is sent off to write a paper on human biology as a branch of science and returns to report that it is the study of arms, legs, heads, and the like; that it also deals with circulation, breathing, and digestion; and that in addition it compares men and women. Such information is certainly something to go by, but it hardly defines the field.[7]

Inkeles, Rose, Williams, and the staff of the Sociological Resources for Secondary Schools project all seem to agree that one needs to look at the methods of inquiry in sociology or at what the sociologist does to the subject matter before an adequate understanding of the nature of the field can be obtained. Further, they believe that some basic notions of social science methods must be taught whenever sociology is taught. But this is easier said than done, for there are some basic disagreements among sociologists related to perceptions of "proper" modes of inquiry for the field. If one gets a group of sociologists together to discuss their field broadly or to discuss a single study within a particular specialization, arguments will almost inevitably develop on basic methodological and related philosophical questions. For example, there is still, after all these years of debate, a sharp disagreement on whether or not sociology can be or should try to become a "pure science." Should it try to be cold and unsympathetic, uninvolved and clinical about social woes; or should sociologists begin their studies with a position, even a zeal, to correct what they regard to be a serious shortcoming in our society? Is sociology, or should it be, a humanistic study? Peter Berger says Yes.[8] Is it more important to expend one's energies building basic

[7] *Ibid.*, pp. 16, 17.
[8] *Invitation to Sociology* (Garden City, N.Y.: Doubleday, 1963).

social theories in the library or in a professor's office, or should one get in the field to gather hard (honest) data? Have certain divisions of sociology, if not the entire field, become so engrossed in playing methodological games that they no longer make a contribution to understanding society? A good many anthropologists tell us this is true of sociology.

If sociologists are *truly* scientific, if they *always* speak conditionally and tentatively, if they offer *all* possible alternatives and consequences, if they look at *all* the evidence, if they control *all* the variables, then are they simply playing a highly intellectualized and phoney game of life? These questions put sociology on the horns of a dilemma: on the one hand, are they complicating and clouding common sense; and, on the other, are they oversimplifying reality? Should sociologists "be men on white horses or men in white coats?" Are they in the middle of life or on the edge or somewhere in between? If in between, then precisely where? Most basic, are there social laws or not? Related to this, can we truly measure human behavior or not? Finally, how do we know if we have an adequate measure?

Joseph Schwab tells us that these issues are common in all disciplines, and that no area knows the answers. He says that in varying degrees every scholar must personally come to grips with these questions, that sociology is only one of many disciplines frustrated by these concerns.[9] But even if Schwab is correct, this information does not help much with the everyday problems of doing sociological research or even reading in the field. Meanwhile the internal battles in sociology are raging.[10]

There is some agreement. There are some modes of in-

[9] "What Do Scientists Do?" *Behavioral Science,* V (1960), 1–27.

[10] Phillip E. Hammond, *Sociologists at Work* (New York: Basic Books, 1964).

quiry which would be accepted by nearly all practicing sociologists, at least, if we do not probe too deeply into what is meant by them. If we can identify some common ground on the nature of method, we might be able to extend our definition.

Rose's little book, which has already been mentioned, is written for public school teachers and other curriculum workers who may not have any sophistication in sociology. Her elementary comments on methodology provide a common ground, and I would, therefore, like to paraphrase them here. She says that the sociologist uses:

1. Questionnaires. These are aimed sometimes at direct, straight-forward responses and sometimes at projected, unconscious, or "hidden" ones.

2. Interviews. These are sometimes in tightly structured short forms and sometimes in long, "free-flowing," open-ended styles.

3. Content analyses. Sometimes these are simple quantifications of, for example, the number of times pejorative adjectives are used in some documents to describe a minority group; at other times this process involves the use of complicated, tightly structured instruments of the check-list variety; still other times the sociologist will "analyze" written materials partially using the tools of the philosopher and of the literary critic.

4. Historical analyses. Sometimes a specific group will be studied historically in order to provide a detailed case study which will offer the opportunity for generalization to other similar cases. At times the scholar will engage in "sociological biography." Full-blown general sociological-historical surveys do occur, but they are not common. Typically, historical methods are used by the sociologist for small depth studies.

5. Laboratory experiments. In some instances, not really

very often, sociologists will establish artificial human situations in a laboratory. They might, for example, stimulate high morale in a specially formed group and then deliberately try to destroy the positive group feelings, all the time carefully observing what is happening. Most sociologists are fairly suspicious of most of this research. They question the "normality" of behavior in such a setting.

6. Observation, including participation. Occasionally, and this practice is probably on the increase, a sociologist tries to join a group, and once he is accepted in it, he steps back and studies the association. This practice requires a highly sophisticated role-playing operation. (Of course, observation of the behavior of a group to which the scholar does not belong is a common technique.) The problem here is to observe without distracting the group—to observe without becoming a significant factor in determining its behavior.

7. Model building. The sociologist may spend his research efforts in building models of types of behavior. He observes and studies complex interactions and then tries to determine a classification system to aid in further research. He is making an effort to categorize human group behavior, eventually for predictive purposes.

In most of these broad research types and procedures the sociologist must be a careful record keeper, and he must understand enough of statistical procedures to speak fairly confidently about whether or not the phenomenon occurred simply on the basis of chance.

I would like to introduce one other interesting and dramatically different typology for sociological research. Professor Paul Lazarsfeld is revising his reader, *The Language of Social Research,* which he edited in conjunction with Morris Rosenberg. The original edition, published in 1955, contained five categories; the new edition will contain eight. The newer ones reflect the trend, according to Lazarsfeld, toward more qualitative research in sociology. His categories are: (1) concepts and indices (the problems of transforming concepts into indices); (2) classifications and typologies (involving coding and logical analyses among other processes); (3) multivariate analysis (studies of relations among variables); (4) characteristics and propositions about groups; (5) studies involving change over time; (6) experimentation; (7) empirical study of action (causal studies—why people act the way they do); and (8) qualitative analysis (nonvariate research, situations in which questionnaires and structured interviews will not work). Again, this outline should call attention to the breadth of the field. In fact, the wide range of topics and methods has sometimes resulted in the argument that sociology is the "organizer," the "coordinator," or the "queen" of the social or behavioral sciences.

Each discipline that has been introduced so far has seemed tremendously broad. The next one, anthropology, will continue the trend. Sociology, however, seems to have a different kind of breadth from history, geography, or anthropology. Perhaps it is just that sociology seems to roam less often from concerns and approaches that are conventionally viewed as belonging to the social sciences. Be this as it may, the scope of sociology is broader, I think, than most people imagine.

Inkeles, after discussing the overlap between the social sciences and the fact that the number of topics of interest to the sociologists continues to expand, concludes by saying:

We may say that sociology is the study of social order, meaning thereby the underlying regularity of human social behavior.

The concept of order includes the efforts to attain it and departures from it. Sociology seeks to define the units of human social action and to discover the pattern in the relation of these units—that is, to learn how they are organized as systems of action. Working with such systems of action, sociology attempts to explain their continuity through time, and to understand how and why these units and their relations change or cease to exist.[11]

Structural Content

The scholars who worked with us were all very reluctant to make any detailed remarks on topics related to when and how content should be handled. As a recognition of the special expertise of public school teachers, their hesitancy was probably inevitable. Our study group, however, regretted that our consultants chose to skirt this subject, since even general suggestions about what to teach must rest on a good many basic pedagogical assumptions, which it is always helpful to understand.

Williams believes that sociological content ought to be taught to all pupils in our elementary and secondary schools, but he too was loath to discuss specific matters related to the teaching of the field in precollege institutions. Persistent questioning, however, did elicit some quite interesting pedagogical comments. Some of his teaching suggestions are outlined in the final section of this chapter. Generally, he does believe sociology as it has been defined here should be taught in conjunction with other subjects and, hopefully, somewhere in the curriculum as a separate discipline. He further believes that a trend to teach more sociology before college is well established. Although data on this matter are difficult to obtain, at least one survey

11 *What is Sociology?* p. 27.

[120]

documents this position by claiming that of the high schools sampled, 24 per cent were offering a separate sociology course in 1963, while 20 per cent were doing so in 1958.[12] It seems only fair for me to add here that I would like to see sociology have a far more important place in the elementary and secondary school curriculum than it has had in the past.

About what content should be taught Williams did not hesitate to be quite specific.[13] He believes that a sociological study of our society must be built on at least an elementary grasp of its historical and geographical foundations. Pupils must have some understanding of the availability of physical resources, the nature of our climate, demographic characteristics, and the history of our commercial, industrial, agricultural, and general economic development. For example, the student should know that our society is and has been an affluent one, and he ought to understand why this is so. Obviously, sociology per se should follow some work in history and geography.

Once the pupil has some basic understanding and appreciation of our physical and historical endowments, he must be led to understand that "human societies as they actually exist are not explainable by any sort of physical or biological determinism." [14] According to Williams, the student at this precise point begins to study sociology. He must realize

[12] Scarvia B. Anderson and others, *Social Studies in Secondary Schools: A Survey of Courses and Practices* (Princeton, N.J.: Educational Testing Service, 1964), p. 12.

[13] The following summary is based mainly on Williams' remarks at Cornell, but I have also borrowed from his *American Society: A Sociological Interpretation* (rev. ed.; New York: Knopf, 1961), a text written for a college course on the general structure and functioning of American society. Chapter 3 is particularly helpful, and parts of it have been paraphrased here.

[14] *Ibid.*, p. 19.

that these endowments provide only a framework for a broad range of possible social adaptations. Sociological ideas help us to understand why particular social alternatives or ways of living have occurred within this range of possibilities. This "nondeterministic" view is the first lesson of sociology. (Again, the similarity to comments made about geography is striking.)

A second foundational idea in the discipline is that human behavior is studiable. That is, there are (1) recurring patterns of behavior which are (2) common to many individuals and groups and (3) significantly related to or associated with other patterns of human thought, feelings, and action. A student of social science, if he is to accomplish anything, must begin his study of man by recognizing that in spite of all the complexity and individuality he observes in human behavior, there are some constant underlying patterns, regularities, norms, rules, laws. "The often repeated question of whether human conduct is really predictable at all is answered every day that a society exists. Without some rough predictability as to what other people will do under given circumstances, there could be no continuing human association, no adjustment, no cooperation." [15] There could also be no social sciences, because man would not be studiable. What social scientist would be willing to argue that there was no such thing as social science?

Moving from these two basic assumptions, Williams identifies a few germinal concepts which must be understood if one is to have an elementary, but essential, grasp of sociology. The first and most significant of these is "culture." Our consultant employed the broadest possible definition of the term, but argued forcefully that its tremendous scope in no way detracts from the usefulness and relevance of the idea.

[15] *Ibid.*, p. 21.

Culture was defined as the "total legacy of past human behavior, effective in the present—social heredity." [16] Artifacts and the know-how involved in their use, knowledge, beliefs, values—the total of man's ways of dealing with his world—this is culture. The student must understand that his culture (1) has developed throughout history, (2) is continually undergoing change at varying rates, (3) must be learned, and because of its complexity, deliberate effort must be made to teach worthy parts of it, and (4) will continue beyond his life span with or without his having made a useful contribution to it. Williams believes that a systematic study of one's own society is the most appropriate way to obtain a true understanding of the meaning of culture.

This belief leads to the next concept. The beginning sociology student needs to give serious attention to the normative aspects of culture. He needs to examine and ascertain the personal significance of the rules for behavior in his society. He must, in short, study the second basic concept, "cultural norm."

Williams lists seven significant ideas which are subsumed under the notion of cultural norm and should be examined even by beginning students: (1) Extent of knowledge regarding the norm.—How many people in the group are aware of the "rule"? (2) Prevalence of acceptance or agreement with the norm. Knowing the norm does not necessarily mean accepting it. How many who know it exists, accept it? (3) Amount and types of people affected by the norm. Who is concerned? (4) Nature and extent of deviance or nonconformity within the norm. How many break the rule? Why? When? (5) Nature of enforcement procedures. What punishment or rewards are used to enforce the rule? Who has the responsibility for enforcement and how did the in-

16 *Ibid.*, p. 22.

dividual or group gain this authority? How consistently is enforcement practiced? What is the degree to which enforcement is internalized by the lawbreaker? (6) Process of transmitting the norm. How is the norm acquired? Where? Who has responsibility for teaching this rule? Why? (7) Nature and form the norm takes. What is the explicitness, the specificity, the rigidity, or the flexibility of the law? Is it written? Where? Understanding cultural norms with these crucial characteristics is essential. Williams suggests that some of these norms should be studied in detail by examining the seven characteristics just cited. He recommends case studies of some particularly interesting norms, not a broad cataloging.

The third major concept is institution. A central and fundamental social goal or need in any society will have norms or rules, processes, and mechanisms clustered around it which have developed to help achieve this objective. The goal and the ways of reaching it are called an "institution." Institutions are classified into at least four major categories: political ones, which are developed around adaptations to the notion of power; economic institutions, which are concerned with the allocation of resources to satisfy material human wants; expressive-integrative institutions, which deal with the transmission and communication of ideas, appreciations, beliefs, attitudes, and technologies; and kinship institutions, which are concerned with sex and child-rearing.

Each of these basic institutions has its own distinct norms and expectations. The cultural norms associated with these fundamental institutions become the more rigid and more widely accepted rules of a society. They are called "institutional norms"; the social sanctions for disobeying them are severe. Most members of a society internalize these norms and conform without much question.

"Institutions regulate the modes of meeting important recurrent situations and at the same time help ensure that the situations will recur. . . . However, within such complex aggregates as modern nations many norms are effective only within limited subcultures, and there are wide differences in individual conformity and conceptions of the normative structure." [17] But institutional norms may lag behind social changes. For example, a majority may become a minority and still unfairly control behavior. Or a minority may not have its rights recognized. Then, too, some few individuals will not conform to even the most fundamental institutional norms. Sometimes the rules of one institution will conflict with those of another. Priorities between norms will vary. These difficulties are perhaps the major deterrents to a completely integrated and equitable society. Williams argues that in order to understand deviance of these types, one must first understand institutional norms.

There are three main problems in the study of social institutions. First, one must describe and analyze the normative structure itself: the existing patterns, their causes and interrelations, the sources and mechanisms of institutional integration, and consequences of the norms. Second, one must discover the processes of change in institutional patterns: their causes, mechanisms, and results. Third, one must study the relation of individual personalities to the normative structure. This is the area of "social psychology" dealing with culture-and-personality problems and facing the complexities of "social control" and of motivations for conforming, innovating, or dissenting.[18]

[17] *Ibid.*, p. 32.   [18] *Ibid.*, pp. 34, 35.

But do not be misled. While our consultant believes it is essential to study the concept of institution, he does not mean that it is desirable to try to examine all of them, nor does he mean that any particular institution necessarily must be studied. The teacher must carefully select one or a few institutions for depth study. Again, the idea of a case study was emphasized.

Two other ideas remain which are basic to understanding culture and cultural norm and are therefore essential in a study of sociology. They have been implied throughout our discussion—one is "status," the other is "role."

There is considerable disagreement among sociologists regarding the precise meaning of these terms, and consequently there are differences of opinion over their specific importance in the structure of the discipline. Williams believes they are vital. He defines status as a position or place in a set of relationships among people. He believes statuses are always polar or reciprocal; one status automatically implies at least one other—teacher-pupil, for example, or lawyer-client. Role for Williams is the expected or anticipated or demanded pattern of behavior associated with a particular status. Certain rights, duties, and/or responsibilities are an integral part of the "assignment" of a status. These functions become the role. The expectations, then, become, in one sense, the meaning of the term. When we say and think of "father," we are usually perceiving the role a father is expected to play in our culture.

Every member of our complex society has many different statuses; therefore each plays different roles. Frequently, the theoretically distinct roles become merged and overlap. For example, when a man makes a decision at the polling place, he frequently is forced to consider the relations between conflicting roles. He is forced to say, for example, How would a father of a young family vote? a local committee chairman of the Democratic party? a teacher? a taxpayer? a debtor? a son of retired and pensioned parents? A very important idea, basic in the study of sociology, is "role strain." This is what emerges when there is conflict between our statuses. These strains can and do become complex indeed. To illustrate, consider the man who is a Negro, a lawyer specializing in corporate taxation, the president of a local N.A.A.C.P. chapter, a resident of an all-white, protestant neighborhood (he wants his children in a "good" school), a Republican, and a Roman Catholic. This is a man with role strain.

According to Williams, additional concepts should be introduced in the study of sociology when and if they become useful tools for examining the structural ideas we have just identified. The concepts will shift depending on the teacher and the subject matter of the cases selected. Williams gave as possibilities: "social organization," "social relationship," and "group" (informal and formal). For Williams these concepts have methodological importance.

These last ideas are of considerably less importance than the concepts identified earlier. It should be emphasized that there are others which could be added to the list and that Williams' suggestions could be deleted without serious consequences. The point being made here is that any well-educated teacher should pick and choose from among the ideas associated with this discipline to select the ones that are most useful in helping his students understand the fundamental or structural ideas. The introduction of the technical language of sociology per se should in any event be kept to a minimum. Only those terms or tools which are truly helpful in a particular class should be selected.

In summary, the structure of sociology is an appreciation

Structure and the Social Studies

for and at least a partial understanding of its basic concepts: culture, cultural norm, institution, status, role, and role strain. In addition, certain technical terms should be included when they are helpful.

Some Ideas on Teaching Sociology

A very interesting discussion followed Professor Williams' presentation. Some of the paraphrased highlights of that discussion are offered here because they provide some additional insights into his ideas regarding the structure of sociology.[19]

Q. When we teach sociology, should we use the actual terms of the discipline—that is, status, role, role strain, et cetera?

A. Emphatically, yes. We underestimate kids all the time. Teachers of the social sciences and history consistently do this, while people in science and mathematics have been far more realistic. Elementary school children can understand the ideas which I have presented. For example, they can most definitely make depth studies of such institutions as the family.

Q. Should anthropology be introduced in the elementary school while the introduction of sociology is postponed until high school?

A. I suppose you are concerned with whether or not we should start with less complex cultures and work up to our own. My bias would be to start right at home in our contemporary culture. I am not at all certain that young children can make the comparisons and transfers called for in anthropological studies. I think anthropology is a specialized branch of sociology. I think anthropologists are sociologists in disguise.

Q. Are there any psycho-social dangers in having a youngster

[19] Williams' speech at Cornell, Nov. 25, 1965.

study his group behavior in an analytical way? Are we going to have sick kids?

A. There may be some upset children, but having dangerously ignorant pupils is worse. Psychology most likely presents more problems on this score.

Q. Should we start social science with psychology or sociology —the individual or the group?

A. Start with the individual-in-the-group. You can't really study the two separately at an early age level. As you would expect, I would emphasize the social-psychological aspects of individual behavior. I am a sociologist.

Q. What are your feelings about the role of history in the social studies program?

A. History should be taught, but it has been overemphasized, particularly recitation and memorization of facts. History too often fails to give the student any conceptual tools for understanding society. Too often the study of history has no central theme or organization principles. It just doesn't give enough help in providing tools of analysis. In addition, it clearly doesn't provide enough help in answering the question: What has been happening of social import in the last six months? We must have a balance of history and the social sciences.

Q. What do you think about the likelihood and desirability of a general integrated social science course—social studies?

A. I am very doubtful that such a course for secondary schools or colleges can be developed or would do the job. We just don't know enough about how fields relate to each other and how to communicate between fields. A separate discipline approach in which relationships are identified seems to be the answer. Separate courses in government, sociology, economics, anthropology and history, plus social studies in the early elementary school should be required. [He added geography later.]

Q. Should we start with basic concepts in each field?

Structure and the Social Studies

A. Yes. But, teachers are going to have to know their specialization very well indeed. One needs to really know the field
in order to decide what ideas are basic.

Q. Do you favor a social problems course for high schools?

A. No. It doesn't give the student an intellectual framework.
It is a hit and miss operation. Furthermore, it lacks the
order and logic of a disciplined approach.

All through the discussion Williams reiterated his belief
that sociology with its way of looking at the world and its
basic ideas ought to be and can be taught to all or nearly all
young people. A required course in the secondary school
would be desirable, coupled with the introduction of sociological ideas elsewhere.

Suggestions for Further Reading

In addition to the items cited in the notes, the reader may
wish to consult these references:

Cole, William E. "Sociology," in *The Social Sciences Foundation of the Social Studies*. Ed. John U. Michaelis and A.
Montgomery Johnston. Boston: Allyn and Bacon, 1965.

Lipset, S. Martin, and Neil Smelser, eds. *Sociology: The Progress of a Decade*. Englewood Cliffs, N.J.: Prentice-Hall, 1961.

Merton, Robert K., Leonard Broom, and Leonard Cottrell.
Sociology Today: Problems and Prospects. New York: Basic
Books, 1959.

Parsons, Talcott, ed. *Theories of Social Change*. 2 vols.; New
York: Free Press, 1961.

The entire series published by Prentice-Hall, Foundations of
Modern Sociology, is enthusiastically recommended. The excellent volume by Alex Inkeles has already been cited. The other
volumes are: Wilbert E. Moore, *Social Change;* Neil J. Smelser,
The Sociology of Economic Life; Patricia Cayo Sexton, *The*

American School; Amitai Etzioni, *Modern Organizations;* William J. Goode, *The Family;* Melvin Tumin, *Social Stratification;* Peter Rossi, *Community Social Structure;* Paul Lazarsfeld, *Theory and Method in the Social Sciences;* Theodore M. Mills, *The Sociology of Groups;* William Kornhauser, *Political Society;* Talcott Parsons, *Societies: Evolutionary and Comparative Perspectives;* and Albert K. Cohen, *Deviance and Control.* Some of these volumes were not actually available at the time of this writing, but the quality of the rest of the series and the reputation of the authors lead me to recommend them all.

[6]

Anthropology

What is anthropology? How does one "do" anthropology? How does this discipline fit into the curriculum revision movement in the social studies? If anthropology has structure, what is one scholar's best guess regarding its substance? The Cornell curriculum study group invited reactions to these questions from Douglas L. Oliver of Harvard. Professor Oliver has been closely associated with revision work in the social studies at Educational Services Incorporated (now the Educational Development Center) and elsewhere. A distinguished ethnologist, one of the country's leading scholars on the Oceanic area of the Pacific, he is a museum curator, a frequent consultant to our government, and the author of numerous studies.

Oliver did not give a lecture. Instead he stimulated a lively seminar based partly on his delightful book *Invitation to Anthropology*,[1] which the study group had been requested to read. This chapter summarizes the results of the seminar and examines some of the literature on the nature

[1] Garden City, N.Y.: Natural History Press, 1964. This chapter leans heavily on this work as well as on an abbreviated earlier version: American Council of Learned Societies and National Council for the Social Studies, *The Social Studies and the Social Sciences* (New York: Harcourt, Brace and World, 1962).

[132]

of anthropology. The reader will find some of Oliver's ideas on the structure of anthropology in a more complete form than can be given here in *Invitation to Anthropology,* which should be read to supplement this chapter.

Nature, Scope, and Purpose of Anthropology

In response to a query about the nature of the field, Professor Oliver effectively shocked the study group by stating, "Anthropology is not a discipline at all. It is a meeting place for many disciplines. Don't try to find boundaries for it. This is a useless and hopeless pastime. In the final analysis anthropology is simply what the people who are trained in the field do—and that stretches a very long way." [2] In part this comment was undoubtedly a device to capture the attention of his audience. But it became clear in the course of the discussion that it was only partly a device; Oliver does think that anthropology is logically separable from other segments of scholarly endeavor. It became equally evident that he believes that the breadth and scope of anthropology is such that conventional definitions for a discipline are inappropriate.

Oliver and nearly all writers I know of on this topic employ one sentence in trying to define the field: "Anthropology is the study of man and his works." The statement is always found in quotation marks, but the author is never given. Perhaps no one is willing to take the blame for this brash, glib, frustrating, but undoubtedly accurate shibboleth. If one tries to be more helpful, one has to say that anthropology includes a study of human biology, primates, race, genetics, human growth and development, anatomy, radiobiology, seriology, physiology, cultural history, prehistory, linguistics, semantics, philology, archaeology, geology,

[2] Feb. 28, 1964.

palaeontology, palaeobotony, geophysics, social structures and organization, personality, motivation, government, law, religion, ethnology, ethnography, the arts, folklore, custom, and much more. Anthropology is all this. It is a residual category. It is a bridger of gaps, an integrator. It is a focus for uniting scholars from many orientations who wish to study humanity systematically. In an essay with a kind of soaring, poetic quality Margaret Mead defends its scope as follows:

Anthropology is a uniquely situated discipline, related in diverse ways to many other disciplines, each of which, in specializing, has also inadvertently helped to fragment the mind of modern man. Anthropology is a humanity, represented in the American Council of Learned Societies, concerned with the arts of language and with the versions that human cultures have given of the definition of man and of man's relationship to the universe; anthropology is a science concerned with discovering and ordering the behaviour of man in culture; anthropology is a biological science, concerned with the physical nature of man, with man's place in evolution, with the way genetic and racial difference, ecological adaptations, growth and maturation, and constitutional differences are implicated in man's culture and achievements; anthropology is a historical discipline concerned with reading the record of man's far past and establishing the links which unite the potsherd and the first inscription on stone, in tying together the threads between pre-literate and literate world wherever the sequence occurs, in Egypt, in China, on Crete or in a modern African state. Anthropology is a social science, although never only a social science, because in anthropology man, as a part of the natural world, as a biological creature, is not separated from man as a consumer or producer, member of a group, or possessor of certain psychological faculties. Anthropology is an art. The research skills which go into good field work are as complex as the skills of a musician or a surgeon; a disciplined awareness of self is as essential.[3]

Miss Mead concludes by saying, "For the anthropologist all of life is his subject matter, with the field the most vivid part of that life." [4] Nearly all anthropologists who are willing to say anything about the nature of the field agree regarding its breadth. Also, they agree that anthropology defies traditional classification systems. Still, the offerings in most college departments of anthropology, the texts, the studies in the field, and the training of researchers lead one to believe that at least two major divisions are recognized: physical anthropology and cultural (social) anthropology. Robert Redfield identifies the division by saying:

Anthropology is organized around an interest in man seen as something with the characteristics of all life and around an interest in man seen as something human—a quality not shaped, or very little shared, with other forms of life. The quality that induces the second polarity—humanity—is manifest in three basic forms: as it appears in individuals (personality), in persisting social groups or societies (culture), and in all socialized members of our species (human nature).[5]

This twofold division is about as far as the community of scholars engaged in this work will permit us to go, although an individual scholar is usually interested in a particular subdivision of the field.

[3] "Anthropology and an Education for the Future," in David G. Mandelbaum and others, *The Teaching of Anthropology* (Berkeley and Los Angeles: University of California Press, 1963), p. 596.

[4] *Ibid.*, p. 603.

[5] Robert Redfield, "Relations of Anthropology to the Social Sciences and Humanities," in Sol Tax, ed., *Anthropology Today: Selection* (Chicago: University of Chicago Press, 1962).

As if this description were not broad enough, there are clear signs that the field is continuing to widen its sphere of interests, not to lessen it. The following are some new or at least recently expanded directions which attest to an increase in scope that contradicts the trend to greater specialization in most of the rest of the academic community:

1. Today there is a greater willingness than in the past to study complex, literate, contemporary societies of the "western" world. For an increasing number of anthropologists, cultures of the entire world are a part of their domain. To be sure, there is some disagreement on this point, which will be described later.

2. Fairly recently many anthropologists have begun to insist on the use of the more precise, controlled, and statistical research methods traditionally employed in sociology and economics. Not that older approaches in anthropology have been abandoned. Quite the contrary is true. But they have been supplemented by a desire for "greater precision." Thus, anthropology students need to have additional training and sophistication. In short, anthropologists have increased their methodological interests and, therefore, added to their burden.

3. A striking increase in the amount of attention given to psychology and particularly to personality has occurred. Mental health seems to be a highly significant "new" interest of anthropologists.

4. The team approach is more and more common. That is, anthropologists work with specialists in various aspects of the study of man and then integrate and unify the work of the group. Although this collaboration may seem to reduce the scope of the field, the approach calls for a fairly high degree of understanding and awareness of the colleague's

way of looking at the world, and so, again, broader interests are demanded.

5. The anthropologist has become more interested in the arts and their form than before. Sophisticated aesthetic matters no longer frighten them.

6. The study of values, moral choice, and motivation for human behavior has always been of concern to the young discipline of anthropology; but, of late, the interest has become stronger or at least writings on the subject have been proportionally increased.

7. In spite of the above six directions, there seems to be an increased demand to search for a unifying theory of human behavior. Every effort to follow the model of other disciplines by subdividing the field into specializations is met with a more determined plea to find this unifying theory. The only way to accomplish this end, argue most anthropologists, is to remain "holistic." No real anthropologist seems to be able to forget that however involved he might become in a study of some specialized aspect of a culture, his prime goal is to understand the totality of man. Sol Tax seems to say this as baldly as possible: "Given a choice between fully understanding one piece of a whole . . . or only half understanding a larger whole, we generally prefer the second." [6] So, again, we see that anthropology is willing to take on new roles but is unwilling to reject old ones.

It is only fair to state that not all anthropologists are entirely pleased about the broadened interests. Oliver, for example, disagrees with a good many other modern anthropologists and claims that the most productive and useful effort for scholars in his field is to concentrate on a small,

[6] Sol Tax, ed., *Horizons of Anthropology* (Chicago: Aldine, 1964), p. 252.

fairly homogenous, nonwestern, preliterate society. He argues that the relative simplicity of this type of culture permits one man to come far closer to grasping the totality of life. That is, one mind—a well and widely trained mind —is more likely to perceive the relationships between various aspects of humanity when he studies a "simple" society; and "it is the relationships which are important." [7] When asked specifically if an anthropologist should study the Puerto Rican ghettos of New York City, he answered in the negative. He did think it might be profitable to have an anthropologist work with others on the problems presented by the interaction of this highly complex subculture, but this seemed to him to be "second-best" anthropology. Sol Tax, in his collection of essays called *Horizons of Anthropology*, takes the opposite view. He specifically recommends, for example, that anthropologists should study why a city is unable to keep itself clean and orderly. He even suggests that the anthropologist can and should be very helpful to a university faculty wishing to improve its organization, not in the indirect sense of providing readings for the faculty on how some tribe deals with organizational questions, but in a direct way—actually doing an anthropological study of the faculty social structure. Tax's position seems to be the more common one today.

Methods

The methods of inquiry used by the anthropologist are perhaps a bit more helpful than his definitions in isolating the unique essence of the field. As we have seen, the anthropologist does many of the same sorts of things done by other researchers. But, in addition, he has some procedures that are almost uniquely his own. While the modern anthropol-

[7] Speech at Cornell, Feb. 28, 1964.

ogist obviously works in laboratories, libraries, and offices and while he does almost as much "card-punching" and "sorting" as do some other researchers, his primary workroom is the field and he nearly always begins his work with a direct study of the objects of his investigation—people and/or their remains. He almost never starts out with a specific well-formulated hypothesis to test; instead, he wants to "see how his subjects live." Pertti Pelto, in his chapter on "Methods of Anthropological Research," provides a helpful guide for examining what the anthropologist does.[8]

Pelto divides the field into archaeology, physical anthropology, linguistics, and social-cultural anthropology. The archaeologist digs. He does so with tedious care. He is interested, at least at first, in everything he finds, because nearly all remains may give him clues regarding human life. He meticulously notes items found together. He photographs, draws, and even makes tape recordings of the process of his diggings. When this phase is finished, he returns to his lab and attempts to date his findings by using a variety of increasingly sophisticated techniques. Biological, geological, chemical, and language clues are sought.

Physical anthropologists also dig, or some of them do, but they are looking specifically for human remains. Other physical anthropologists work with living beings. They are interested in all the external and internal characteristics of man, his measurements and coloration, the composition and types of his body fluids, and so on. Genetics and racial characteristics are of tremendous importance to them.

As a linguist, the anthropologist uses a number of mechanical devices—all kinds of recorders, computers,

[8] Pertti J. Pelto, *The Study of Anthropology* (Columbus, Ohio: Merrill, 1965).

television—in his study of language. He attempts to find families of languages. He is interested in the "completeness" and the adequacy of languages and in the similarities and differences among them. In the field he nearly always attempts to learn the local language well enough to communicate, even think in the idiom of the people he is studying. He is interested in the derivation of words and in the formation of the symbols and their combinations that man employs.

The social or cultural anthropologist nearly always lives with his subjects. He interviews, he even uses questionnaires when they are appropriate; more important, he observes. He records everything he sees and hears that might have any significance. He must be careful not to allow his close association with his subjects to cause him to accept what he sees without attaching appropriate significance to it. He must also, of course, learn how to live and participate in the lives of a people without becoming an influencing factor in their daily routines. That is, he must either write himself into a study or, at the very least, be continually aware that his presence is a unique feature in the lives of his subjects. This requirement obviously poses a dilemma, for most anthropologists try to experience as completely as possible the everyday and the unusual aspects of the society they are studying.

While he is in the field, the cultural or social anthropologist gathers concrete information where and when he can— for example, demographic facts, specific details regarding the kinship system, economic data on sources of income, numbers engaged in various ways of making a living, percentages involved in specific social practices. He also keeps a kind of diary in which he records exactly as they happen observations of social interactions of all sorts. He collects statements, written but mostly spoken, in the vernacular of the objects of his study. (A knowledge of the subjects' language seems to be a universally accepted criterion of sound anthropological scholarship.)

When the anthropologist returns from the field, he begins the vital work of analyzing his findings. He employs cross-cultural comparisons and systematically reviews the work done by others. He checks and rechecks his own observations searching for valid and significant relationships. He frequently returns to the site of his investigation for reliability checks. He hopes others will go to his locale. He then begins to write. More like history than geography in this regard, the style of writing seems to be of tremendous importance. In the end he only claims tentative findings.

We see that just as the anthropologist's subject matter is broad and integrative, so are his techniques. "It is probable that anthropology will continue to combine some of the descriptive, holistic methods of the humanities with the more analytic and statistically-oriented practices of the social sciences." [9]

In summary, anthropology tries to be the total study of man. It postulates that all men are worthy of study and that they are the product of the interaction of physical, biological, and cultural factors. The true understanding of man depends on one student's looking at all the factors together at the same time. Anthropologists believe that study of this sort will provide the student with an awareness of other people and other ways of behaving, with a deeper understanding of himself, with a clearer notion of his own role in society, with a basic understanding of the nature of cultural stability and change—in short, with a more profound respect for the dignity of man.

[9] *Ibid.*, p. 48.

Structure and the Social Studies

Perhaps the most appropriate summary of these opening remarks is Kluckhohn's classic statement: "Anthropology holds up a great mirror to man and lets him look at himself in his infinite variety." [10]

Structure

We have already said that the methods of inquiry in a field are a part of its structure; that anthropology is a distinct discipline in large part because of its unique methodology; that its methods include humanistic, nonscientific, nonrepeatable, nonverifiable techniques; and that history, which I believe is even more humanistic, does not have structure because of its lack of an explicit and precise methodology. Now then, does or can anthropology have structure? I think the answer to this question depends on the degree to which the practitioners in the field will abide by the "rules" of science. Anthropologists differ sharply on this matter. Oliver's position seems to be that the field can be structured; however, he refused to say so explicitly. There is no doubt that he provides us with a conceptual structure, but the methodological phase is fairly obscure. Methods and relations among concepts seem to be implied. The following discussion is, I believe, one attempt worthy of our serious consideration at structuring anthropology. This structure is based exclusively on Oliver's remarks at Cornell and on his *Invitation to Anthropology*.

The first idea that Oliver discussed was that humans have many habitual ways of behaving (as distinguished from "once-in-a-lifetime" or random acts). In an unusual application of the term, he calls these recurrent bits of behavior

[10] Clyde Kluckhohn, *Mirror for Man: The Relationship of Anthropology to Modern Life* (New York: McGraw-Hill, 1949), p. 11.

"habits." He states that some habits are learned and others inherited. The student must understand the nature, source, and consequences of habits. He must be exposed to the problem of deciding which habits are learned and which are mainly genetically determined. He must begin to analyze and question his own habits. He must begin to see the efficiencies but also the prejudices which develop from our dependence on automatic or nonrational ways of behaving. He must see that even so-called rational behavior is profoundly affected by habits. He also must consider the degree to which habits are universal or particular.

Then the student must be taught to question the effect of the physical and biotic environment on man. Oliver reminds us that early anthropological studies were largely deterministic. They used such terms as "tropical island cultures" as if all tropical islands were alike. Today, however, anthropology stresses that physical and biotic resources place only some rather tentative parameters on life and that they provide a very large margin for variation. (There seems to be implicit in his argument the belief that modern anthropology avoids, or more nearly avoids, the deterministic attitude that so easily occurs when one thinks exclusively in geographic or economic or political terms. The anthropologist must keep the total spectrum of forces in mind. Whether this is the case or not, Oliver heatedly and repeatedly warned against determinism in all forms.) The ways in which cultural changes affect the influence of physical and biotic features must be explored. In Oliver's view, this, like most other concepts of anthropology, can best be understood by having students examine a particular society in some depth; which one they study does not really seem to matter so much. The important thing is for them to perceive, for example, that the effect of the annual rainfall of a region is profoundly influenced by the stage in the development of irrigation procedures that has been achieved.

The student must be led to understand the impact of demographic data on the culture of a people. How many people are there, what is the sexual distribution, how much movement is there and where does this movement take place, how densely are the people living together, what is the shape of the age profile of the community—the answers to these questions are fundamental in most instances to the understanding of a culture. Oliver does not seem to be so much interested in having students know the answers to these questions for any particular culture, but rather to know that the questions must be asked.

Another essential anthropological concept is race. Students must ask what the meaning of race is, what its causes are and its consequences. Race for Oliver is a system for classifying people based on a combination of physical traits genetically determined, but its impact is cultural. The student must be taught to see why this is so. The fact that anthropologists do not agree on the precise criteria for determining race must be made clear, as must the reasons for the disagreement. Students should be aware of the various typologies. They should understand that the distinctions among races "involve differences in total genetic composition of 10 per cent or less." [11] They must be led to ponder the significance or, perhaps better put, the insignificance of these differences. Oliver wants to have students avoid the extremes both of racism and of the ignoring of race. The role of natural selection in determining the races should be studied. Our appalling ignorance regarding race should be made clear. Why we know so little about race should also be

[11] Oliver, *Invitation to Anthropology*, p. 15.

[144]

explored. That is, for example, it should be known that we cannot be certain about some alleged racial difference because we do not know how to measure the capabilities in which we are interested. The fact that cultural bias greatly clouds our judgment should also be made explicit.

Anthropology is also interested in the manufacturing process of a culture, its technology. In anthropological terms technology includes the physical objects needed to make other objects as well as the know-how and even the superstitions associated with production. The student must be led to ask the following questions regarding the essential concept of technology: "What the artifact [the product of the technology] is in terms of its composition, end-use, number in existence, etc. How it is processed; the technical knowledge back of its processing, the tools and forms of energy utilized, the sequence of actions (including magical actions) involved. Where the action is carried out (e.g., settlement patterns, land-use maps). When? (E.g., For two hours every day? During the rainy season? Every ten years?) Who does it? (E.g., Females only, working individually? Groups of young males? Full-time specialists?) " [12] Oliver considers technology in this broad sense to be of tremendous importance in understanding a people, but quite consistently he warns against determinism—this time technological determinism. A key factor here is knowing the significance of the percentage of time and energy that must be expended to obtain food and shelter. How much "excess" time is there and what is done with it?

Ideology—credos, beliefs, ethics, morals, philosophies, goals, orientations, values, "thought-habits"—is another fundamental concept of the field. Oliver stresses the distinction between the ideologies that exist and those that are be-

[12] *Ibid.,* p. 19.

lieved to be desirable. (This distinction and particularly his terminology for it are fairly unusual.) He calls the first set of ideas about the way things are and how they got that way and how they will become "suppositions." The ideas about the way things ought to be he calls "norms." He classifies norms and suppositions in terms of their degree of acceptance, the form they take, and the degree to which they are explicit. The significance of a study of values is tremendous; values are "mankind's most distinctive and crucial habit systems, [essential] to scientific study." The ways in which they are formed, the rationale on which they rest, their consequences—these are at the heart of anthropological study. Oliver wants even very young students to think about a culture in terms of its ideologies, and claims that a study of a society without considering this aspect is incomplete and almost useless.

Closely related to an understanding of the values of men is an understanding of their language. Students need to explore the concept of language—the working vocabulary, the grammar, the translatability, nonverbal communication, and the written symbols of a people. Young students cannot be expected to understand completely their own language let alone the languages of others, but they must be taught very early to perceive the significance of language and to raise questions about it whenever they try to understand a people. It is important to study the human and nonhuman functions of languages, their similarities and differences.

An additional family of essential concepts has to do with social relations. These concepts are, of course, related to the ideas that have already been identified. Social relations are derived from the physical, biological, and ideological factors that we have noted. Kinship patterns, religious practices, taboos, power and authority structures or governments, law systems, and the social stratification system are a few of the most important ideas included in the social relations category. Students need to study these concepts, ask questions about them, each time they try to understand a culture. They must see the universal and particular functions and consequences of these vital aspects of social relations.

Underlying the concepts of social relations that have just been identified is the basic need of all men in all times for sociality. The group associations of men must be analyzed. Why do men join or fail to join certain groups? What primary and secondary groups exist in a culture? Why? How are groups similar and different in various societies? How does one go about comparing groups in both inter- and intra-cultural situations? These are the questions that must be asked.

Personality is an anthropological concept of great importance. This statement may surprise the reader, because personality is traditionally considered to be among the basic topics in psychology. But it should be clear by now that anthropology has "borrowed" nearly all its concepts; it is only the integration of them that is unique. The anthropologist is interested in both individual personalities—Oliver believes that anthropological interest in this topic is only about forty years old—and in group personalities. The latter idea is, of course, fraught with danger; it can easily lead the unsophisticated to stereotyped thinking. Oliver takes Ruth Benedict and other colleagues to task for their efforts to "personalize" cultures and then almost willy-nilly assign these traits to the individual personalities of the people living in the culture. Still, our consultant argues that tentative formulations along these lines are extremely valuable in trying to understand a culture. The student should examine "descriptive generalizations concerning the types of individuals predominating in particular societies, in terms of their 'psychological' habits; explanations of why individuals in different societies differ in these respects or, looked at the other way around, how 'personalities' become shaped by their social milieus; and more sophisticated statements about the 'psychic unity of mankind.' " [13] The basic value involved in this study is to perceive the ways in which culture and personality are associated.

Another group of structural concepts can be classified under the term "culture change." Oliver distinguishes between two basic types of interests in this topic: cycles of change both for individuals and communities, and the non-cyclical process of innovation and diffusion. The first category is concerned with the ritualizations, rites, and customs associated with important physiological and cultural events —for example, birth, puberty, marriage, patriotic occasions, death, introduction into occupations. It is also concerned with the weekly, monthly, and yearly cycles of cultural events in communities: holidays, seasonal customs, days for particular work, planting time. The other part of the category, and probably the more important, has to do with how a community (and an individual) adapts to change. Oliver reminds us that cultural evolutionism—the belief that all cultures necessarily go through specific stages of development in a particular order—has been rejected, that "historical determinism" is as faulty as geographic or economic determinism. But the anthropologist is nevertheless vitally concerned with the acculturation process. He wants to know what happens to a society when innovation and diffusion take place. He is interested in how this process is altered when the changes are deliberately planned as in a newly "developing" nation striving for rapid transformation. How

[13] *Ibid.*, p. 56.

does the speed of the transformation affect the nature of the cultural change? What or who are the agents of change? Why do people typically resist change even when it is demonstrably good for them? Students need to be led to seek answers to these questions in studying any culture.

Closely related to these ideas are the ones from prehistory. Oliver believes that a crucial element in understanding man is an awareness of his prehistorical heritage. Important stages in the development of man—the use of fire, animal domestication, tool production of evolving types, food production, and so on—ought to be studied. The student ought also to have at least an elementary understanding of the development of the physical characteristics that make him a unique species, or at least unique in terms of some taxonomic systems. In this regard it is important to study the variables which set humanity apart— certain functions of language, incest taboos, particular uses of tools, for example.

All these concepts which we have briefly identified can be summarized, albeit imperfectly, in perhaps the only distinctly anthropological concept—culture. This term has been used throughout the chapter without being defined; one cannot talk about anthropology and fail to use it. We have seen that both geographers and sociologists also regard the notion of culture as absolutely basic to their areas. Certainly, however, wherever else it may belong, culture is the focus of anthropology. Yet the term is a fuzzy one. Oliver's definition of culture seems to be that it is the combination of those learned characteristics that provide a basis for separating human beings into distinguishable groups. Anthropologists do not agree on exactly where to draw boundaries around the meaning of this word, but they all seem to include a wide range of associated phenomena which make a specific group unique. Perhaps a paragraph from Oliver will make this matter a bit more clear.

The word "culture" is perhaps anthropologists' most distinctive word; how confusing therefore that there should be such vagueness and such difference of opinion over what it means. Most commonly, reference in theoretical writings is to learned habits shared by members of the kinds of communities or tribes we have been discussing [relatively "primitive" ones]. But within this broad definition there are many different usages. Anthropologists differ concerning the "level of reality" of habits included in their usage of "culture"—some including all levels, other only normative or normative and suppositional. Others differ over the loci of reference—some refer only to those habits or combinations of habits distinctive of the communities studied, others include all habits stated by the communities in question, including their "universal" habits as well. Again, some writers would include under "culture" not only habits but the material products of such habits—not only the method of shaping an arrowhead but the arrowhead itself (i.e., "material culture") .[14]

One of the valuable lessons of anthropology is for students to come to grips with the difficulty of determining a precise definition for this term and at the same time an appreciation for the value of trying to do so.

In summary, the conceptual structure of anthropology in Oliver's view includes an understanding of habits, the relationships between physical and biotic features of the environment and social and psychological aspects of a society, culture change, population, race, technology, ideology, language, social relations, personality, pre-history (early development of both a biological and cultural sort) , and the all-

14 *Ibid.,* pp. 51–52.

inclusive capstone idea, culture. Oliver did not discuss the methodological phase of structure in any detail.

Curriculum Problems

In Oliver's view anthropology per se should not be taught in elementary or secondary schools. In fact, he says, "I would rather see anthropology not taught as a subject until the last two years of college." [15] He believes that the work he is doing for Educational Services Incorporated (now E.D.C.) is not anthropology per se. (This statement, frankly, adds to my confusion, for this program up to the seventh grade certainly looks like anthropology to me.) In any event what Oliver wants, he says, is the introduction of anthropological examples, ideas, and ways of thinking and working into the total program. For instance, if the teacher wants to introduce his class to the nature and purpose of government, he might well do so by having the children study a society without the kind of controls that a modern complex industrial society has. They should be led to see that the kind of government a society has is based on a complex set of factors. Oliver believes that a study of prehistory is an excellent vehicle for giving the students a basic understanding regarding the need for government and the kinds of government which can be and have developed. Because the pre-college curriculum is already crowded, and because very few teachers in the early school have had formal training in anthropology, and because anthropologists are going through the "pangs of an identity crisis," and because of the holistic nature of the field, he sees no chance of, and little value in, adding courses in anthropology. In short, "the study of anthropology [as a separate course] should be designed mainly for people who are going to become practi-

[15] Speech at Cornell, Feb. 28, 1964.

tioners in the discipline." [16] Further, it should occur mainly in graduate schools.

Assuming that this view is correct, some of the very significant curriculum problems associated with teaching even a small amount of anthropological content remain. Even if anthropology is not taught as a separate course in elementary and secondary schools, if, as Oliver suggests, the curriculum worker and the teacher set out to "infiltrate all of the teaching in our schools with the points of view, methods and findings that come out of the work of anthropology," then there are some serious curriculum problems which must be considered. No attempt to resolve these issues will be made here, but they should be explicitly raised. Parenthetically, as this list of problems unfolds, the reader should be aware of the many similarities with the methodological and organization questions raised in the chapter on geography.

The first and most significant point was made again and again in the opening section of this chapter. I will merely mention it here and hurry on. Anthropology has almost a completely boundless scope and breadth. I am aware, of course, that I made this same point when we were discussing history and geography and even to a lesser degree sociology, but each of these disciplines has some way to limit its scope. Anthropology seems to have none. Which culture(s) should we study? It does not help much to say that it does not matter—one or more must be selected. Some rational means for selection must exist. Some cultures must provide better examples than others. What should be studied about a culture once it has been selected? If we accept anthropology as its face value, we must study all factors. How much time will

16 *Ibid.*

thus be consumed? Do younger teachers and even experienced ones need a tighter framework, a more rigid disciplinary support, to give them direction and guidance?

Then there is the fact that social studies teachers have not studied anthropology. There are no recent precise figures on this matter, but one can get a feel for the problem by noting that many of the colleges which train large numbers of teachers do not even have anthropology departments. Further, it has been my experience that even where excellent anthropology departments exist, very few prospective teachers take the courses. I would estimate that no more than one per cent of our recent graduates in teacher education at Cornell University have had a major in anthropology and no more than 8 per cent have ever had a course in the field. How can a culture be studied anthropologically or how even can the "anthropological point of view" be introduced when the teachers have never studied the field?

There is also a problem that exists, to be sure, in any discipline but that seems particularly troublesome in this field. The issue is keeping the subject matter in its proper perspective. It would be and has been very easy to fall into a trap in teaching anthropological content in which the relatively unimportant details of a "primitive" culture study become an end in themselves while the generalizations and transferability of the subject are lost. The worst form of antiquarianism could easily occur. Relatively unimportant but complex details in the broad scheme of things could become tremendously important in trying to understand the tribe under study. To be sure, this is not a necessary result of studying anthropology, but it is a very plausible one.

Oliver and the other anthropologists I have read have lamented the imprecision of their analytic tools. If this fact

is troublesome for them, it is undoubtedly even more difficult for the unsophisticated precollege teacher. It can lead
to a serious situation in which students fail to see the necessity for at least seeking to communicate clearly and defini-
tively. It is one thing—and a good thing—for students to
appreciate the difficulty of giving precise meaning to culture, community, race, and so on; it is another thing—and a
bad thing—for them to accept this imprecision as a fact
without a concomitant appreciation of the need to continue
to seek clarity.

In summary, there is the possibility that a necessarily imperfect and incomplete introduction of some of the concepts
and approaches of anthropology to the unsophisticated by
the unsophisticated might lead to uncritical, unscientific,
emotionalized thinking about man or to a study of insignificant societies for their own sake. Further, the introduction
of the study of anthropology in elementary schools would
mean the reduction of the time now devoted to contemporary societies. Yet, at the same time, we are seeing an unmis-
takable trend to introduce more "cultural studies" into the
curriculum. We are hearing a good many people suggest
that anthropology ought to replace history as the organizing
discipline of the social studies. (Make no mistake, Oliver
did not say this.) Where will this lead? Where should it
lead? This is a vitally important matter for curriculum
workers in the social studies to study and resolve. Perhaps
the "answer" is that there is no single answer, that there
ought to be several ways to organize the curriculum and
teachers should take their choice. We probably should not
leave this subject without saying that geography and sociology might provide the discipline framework for a culturally
based social studies program as well as anthropology.

Suggestions for Further Reading

As I indicated in Chapter 1, there are a number of curriculum studies underway that are focused at least partly on anthropology. The materials being produced by these projects are of considerable interest. Three of the most significant in this category are:

Anthropology Curriculum Study Project, Malcolm Collier, Director, 5632 Kimbark Avenue, Chicago, Illinois 60637

Anthropology Curriculum Project, Wilfrid C. Bailey, Director, University of Georgia, Peabody Hall, Athens, Georgia 30601

Educational Development Corporation, 15 Mifflin Place, Cambridge, Massachusetts

In addition to the items cited above and in the notes, the reader may find the following materials helpful:

Brown, Ina Corrine. *Understanding Other Cultures.* Englewood Cliffs, N.J.: Prentice-Hall, 1963.

Fried, Morton H. *Readings in Anthropology.* 2 vols.; New York: Crowell, 1958.

Goldschmidt, Walter. *Exploring the Ways of Mankind.* New York: Holt, Rinehart and Winston, 1960.

Goodenough, Ward. *Cooperation in Change.* New York: Russell Sage Foundation, 1963.

Kroeber, A. L. *Anthropology, Biology, and Race* and *Anthropology: Culture Patterns and Processes.* New York: Harbinger, 1963.

Powdermaker, Hortense. *Stranger and Friend: The Way of an Anthropologist.* New York: Norton, 1966. See particularly the epilogue.

[7]

Economics

As we indicated before, it is almost commonplace today to find first-rate scholars in nearly all fields, including the social sciences and history, thinking and writing about the elementary and secondary school curriculum. But long before this practice was fashionable in most subject areas, it was happening in economics. For example, the highly influential Joint Council on Economic Education was founded in 1948. Its major purpose was and is the improvement of the teaching of economics. From the start, the group has had the active support of outstanding professional economists and educators, as well as leaders from industry, labor, government, agriculture, business, and consumer organizations. And even before the J.C.E.E. was organized, a number of nationally recognized economists were working on the elementary and secondary school curriculum. One such economist, who is currently a leader in economics education and who has spent a good part of his professional life in a study of the teaching of economics, is Laurence Leamer from the State University of New York at Binghamton (Harpur College). We were honored to have him serve as our consultant.

Leamer's presentation and the discussion that followed

were almost entirely focused on the substantive structure of economics—what economic content should be taught to all children in elementary and secondary schools. Quite a spirited discussion accompanied some of the specific recommendations, and we will turn to it later. Leamer's remarks at Cornell did not deal with some of the significant questions which are involved in structuring a discipline for curriculum purposes, such questions as: How should the discipline be defined? What are the problems of teaching it? How should the field be organized for research and teaching? What are the purposes of the field? To be sure, all these matters were considered indirectly while attacking the problem of what should be taught. Still, we should be more direct here. Fortunately, there is a considerable literature on these questions, including the views of Professor Leamer.

A Definition

In a booklet written as a text for secondary school pupils, Leamer says:

The two striking facts about our economy—countless unsatisfied wants in the presence of great abundance—form the starting point of economic inquiry. To assist our understanding of how we have organized to produce abundance is the descriptive purpose of economics. To assist our discovery of how we may better organize to satisfy more of our unsatisfied wants is the practical purpose of economics.[1]

At a later point in this same publication, Leamer describes the field of economics as being concerned with four basic questions: (1) what and how much consumer goods should

[1] Laurence E. Leamer and Dorothy Lampen Thompson, *American Capitalism: An Introduction for Young Citizens* (Washington, D.C.: Council for the Advancement of Secondary Education, 1958), p. 2.

be produced, (2) what and how much capital goods should be produced, (3) how resources for the production of all these goods should be organized, (4) and which consumers should receive the goods.[2] We find these questions in slightly different form again and again in the literature. For example, Paul Samuelson shortens them to: Production—what, how much, and for whom?[3] Some economists would add, Who makes these economic decisions and how and why are they made? Certainly, this last issue is an important part of economics even though it overlaps with the field of government and other areas. Although the question is rarely included in a list of the basic dilemmas for the field, it is almost always discussed in basic economics texts for all levels. In any event, these few questions having to do with the allocation of resources are frequently offered as a definition for the field.

To return to definitions phrased in a more conventional format, the English economist Alfred Marshall is widely quoted as follows:

Political economy or economics is a study of mankind in the ordinary business of life; it examines that part of the individual and social action which is most closely connected with the attainment and with the use of the material requisites of well-being.[4]

One of the leading texts for introductory college courses in this field is *Economics: An Introduction to Analysis and Policy* by George Leland Bach. The opening two paragraphs of this book are very helpful in clarifying the meaning of the field as a whole and of its two major parts:

[2] *Ibid.*, p. 6.   [3] *Economics* (New York: McGraw-Hill, 1948).
[4] *Principles of Economics* (New York: Macmillan, 1948), p. 1.

Economics is the study of how the economic system produces the goods and services we want, and how it distributes them among us (economic analysis). Equally it is concerned with how we can make the system work better (economic policy). Economic analysis is a necessary foundation for sound economic policy.

Economists usually look at the economic system in two ways. One way is to look at its behavior in the aggregate—at booms and depressions, at total production and the rate of economic growth, at the total supply of money, at total purchasing power in relation to the goods available, at inflation and deflation. This approach they call "macro economics," since macro means large or whole. The other way is to look at the individual businesses and people who underlie the aggregates of macro economics. This involves studying how individuals (consumers) spend their money; how business concerns respond to consumer demands; how individual wages and salaries are determined; how big businesses compare with little businesses; and so on. This approach economists call "micro economics," since micro implies emphasis on the individual parts of the system.[5]

Purposes of Teaching Economics

In operational terms it is impossible to make a sharp distinction between the definition for a field and the purposes for teaching and studying it. A good definition prescribes objectives. Partly for this reason most of the essays of this book have not specifically dealt with teaching objectives. In this instance, however, examining a statement of goals seems to help to sharpen the ideas on the conceptual structure.

In an article discussing the desirable contribution of economics to the general education of college students,[6]

[5] Englewood Cliffs, N.J.: Prentice-Hall, 1954, pp. 3–4.
[6] "Philosophy of Economic Education," *Atlanta Economic Review*, IX (June 1959), 12.

John Chalmers and Professor Leamer outlined four basic objectives, which may be summarized as follows:

1. The primary purpose of teaching economics is to give students a fundamental knowledge of our socioeconomic organization. In discussing this point, the authors seem to be particularly interested in making clear to the students that our economic organization is determined by free markets *plus* customs, public decisions, and controls or authorities of a variety of types, but primarily governmental. They claim further that the best way to teach the "facts of life" regarding our socioeconomic organization at the college level is to use comparisons. Students first need to be shown that all societies have to solve the same basic economic questions. Then, to understand and appreciate our particular procedures for solving these questions, the student should become involved in a comparison of the means that have been used in various systems to attack these problems.

2. The second major reason for including economics in the general education of college students, according to Chalmers and Leamer, is to provide them with the understandings necessary to participate intelligently in public decisions regarding the political and economic problems of citizenship in our society. Participation presumably involves action at the voting place or elsewhere when it is appropriate. The authors claim that the relationship between matters that are traditionally viewed as economic affairs and the other important factors involved in citizenship should be emphasized.

3. The third objective is to help students get the background necessary for intelligent participation in public discussions of specific economic problems. There is obviously a close relationship to the preceding point here, but the authors claim that a significant difference exists. The distinc-

tion involves a different subject matter and not a dissimilar method.

4. Finally, the students should be taught to use economic reasoning or the methods of the economist. Again, this fourth objective is related to the others. Economic reasoning obviously would be involved in becoming an informed active citizen. The point is, I believe, that we need to emphasize both content and methodological objectives.

The degree of emphasis on this methodological phase of teaching economics varies, of course, from statement to statement; but it is fair to say that developing the ability and desire to think critically or rationally about economic questions is by far the most commonly stated objective for this field. Just as Leamer has made economic problems, associated political and social problems, and the process of solving them three-fourths of his purpose statement for teaching economics, so would most of the other economists who are speaking on this question. Economic reasoning is the primary goal.

This is probably a good place in this discourse to identify some of the major misconceptions about the purpose of economics. First, the field does not attempt to provide a recipe for dealing with the major value questions of life. It hopes to help man assess accurately the cost and consequences of various courses of action. It emphasizes that man must continually be aware of the ways in which his values color his decisions. It does not tell him to ignore his values. It emphasizes that decisions that are not entirely rational are made continually by all of us. But economics is not centered on values; it does not deal with the ultimate meaning of life, nor do its proponents make this claim. There are still a few economists who say the field should be absolutely value-free; most of them do not want to go this far. Nearly all agree that only the zealot looks at all matters with the blinders provided by an exclusively economic orientation. Narrow materialism and determinism are not consistent with economic reasoning. Values must enter the picture, but when you study them per se you are no longer studying economics.

Also, the field is not a how-to-do-it subject. It is primarily theoretical. The discipline is not focused on immediate utility. If you want to learn how to run a business, or buy a mattress, or manage a home, or balance your checkbook, or build a school, or run a fund-raising campaign, you should not hurry to the nearest college to enroll in an extension course in economics. Business administration, home economics, consumer economics, accounting, and the rest are partially built on economic principles, but they are not economics. (Incidentally, most of the professionals in the subjects just named would claim to be theoretically oriented also.) Nevertheless, economists are quite chagrined at labeling as economics a course primarily aimed at any of the skills listed above.

A final statement of purpose for studying economics, which says basically the same thing that Leamer said, but seems to make the point in a somewhat more forceful way, occurs at the conclusion of an excellent book on economic education by Richard Martin and Reuben Miller:

The basic economic problem of scarcity can never be solved once and for all. In our dynamic world we are constantly being confronted with new situations, new problems, new knowledge, new potentials, and new aspirations which require continuous adjustment and readjustment in economic matters. Economic understanding is necessary if we are to deal intelligently with these changes.

In order to live harmoniously in society, an individual should have both reasonable knowledge of the operations of the economic system, a clear recognition of the goals he wants to achieve, and make a reasoned choice of the line of action which will best achieve individual and social goals. A knowledge of economics permits the individual citizen to recognize those parts of economic questions for which a "scientific" answer is possible, those for which such answers are impossible because the necessary information or data are unavailable, and those where value judgments are unavoidable.[7]

This, then, is what economics is and what it is trying to do.

Organization

It seems necessary to explore one final matter concerning the nature of economics before we turn to its structure. How is the discipline organized to serve the purposes just enumerated? What are its subdivisions or specializations which exist to help the teacher and researcher narrow the scope of the field? We have already seen that the field has been divided into two large areas, micro- and macro-economics. But further division is necessary to make the field manageable.

Leamer and Percy L. Guyton, an economist who is working for the Joint Council on Economic Education, have recently published a useful guide for schools that are trying to develop a library in economics.[8] The authors divide the books and other instructional materials for the field into a simple classification system. To be sure, there is some over-

[7] *Economics and Its Significance* (Columbus, Ohio: Merrill, 1965), pp. 84–85.

[8] *Suggestions for a Basic Economics Library* (rev. ed.; New York: Joint Council on Economic Education, 1965), pp. iii–iv.

lap, and some topics will not fit neatly and completely into the categories provided, but it is a simple system which is understandable to a noneconomist. Here is their plan: 0. Economics, general (materials that deal with the whole sweep of the field). 1. Economic theory and analysis—1.0 general, 1.1 micro, 1.2 macro, 1.3 mathematical and statistical analysis. 2. Economic systems (subdivided into the conventional "isms"). 3. History of economic thought (concerned with the development of the discipline). 4. Economic history (subdivided into various national economic histories). 5. Economic goals—5.0 general, 5.1 economic growth and development, 5.2 economic stability, 5.3 economic equity, 5.4 economic security. 6. Economic resources—6.0 general, 6.1 natural, 6.2 human, 6.3 capital, 6.4 knowledge and technology. 7. Economic sectors—7.0 general, 7.1 business, 7.2 agriculture, 7.3 labor, 7.4 consumers, 7.5 financial institutions, 7.6 government, 7.7 international. 8. Economic area studies: economic geography. 9. Economic education (questions related to teaching economics).

The more traditional classification system of economics is provided by the division for membership in the American Economics Association. The sixteen major classes are: 1. General economic theory. 2. Economic history. 3. Economic development; national economics. 4. Economic statistics. 5. Economic systems; planning and reform; cooperation. 6. Business fluctuations. 7. Money credit and banking. 8. Public finance; fiscal policy. 9. International economics. 10. Business finance; investment and securities markets. 11. Business administration; marketing and accounting. 12. Industrial organization; government and business; industry studies. 13. Land economics; agricultural economics; economic geography; housing. 14. Labor economics. 15. Population; welfare programs; standards of living. 16. Related disciplines.

Both these organization plans can be distilled into four broad categories: economic theory, economic policy, economic measurement and methodology, and economic history. Economic theorists are concerned with developing principles and generalizations which explain human behavior as it is related to the production and consumption of items desired for the satisfaction of material wants. Economic policy is that segment of the discipline that is concerned with action—the steps that can and should be taken by various sectors of the economy including the government to achieve desired results. The third category speaks for itself. (Parenthetically, econometrics is the fastest growing division of the field.) More or less accurate measurements of the rates of changes and other phenomena are essential for prediction, in fact for the whole policy area. Finally, like almost every other branch of knowledge, economics is interested in checking the situation of the present and expectations for the future against what is known of the past—this is economic history.

Now let us turn to the content from these four areas which Leamer believes should be taught to all.

Structure

Leamer's views on the essential content of economics are stated here almost entirely as he wrote them.

The economic problem. Economics begins from the fact that men's wants exceed their ability to satisfy them, that resources are scarce in relation to uses to which they must be put if men's wants are to be fulfilled. The discipline of economics takes men's wants as given and concentrates on alleviating the economic problem by the best use of resources. The ways in which men try to solve the economic problem may be conveniently grouped under three different though interrelated sets of ideas—production, allocation, and economic systems.

Production and its determinants. Production involves the converting of scarce resources into desired goods and services. To understand the general nature of production one must understand its determinants, including the factors of production, their quantity and quality, division of labor, the role of savings, investment and capital formation, diminishing returns, and finally the importance of the allocation of resources and the economic system (the next two topics).

Allocation of resources and economic choice. This is probably the most fundamental set of ideas in economics; it is the essence of economizing. To economize is to so allocate (use) all scarce transferable resources in their alternate possible uses that the maximum total product of desired goods and services is secured. The economic principle provides our guidelines to optimum allocation; resources should be so used that a unit of the resource will produce an equally valuable additional product in all alternative possible uses. The opportunity cost principle is a guideline for choice derived from the basic economic principle. That is, the scarce transferable resources should be "spent" to create a product that is desired more than the alternatives which would have consumed the same resources. This principle is the unique potential contribution of economics to reasoning and choice; economics, I believe, offers the most effective subject matter through which to teach this basic principle. Wherever and whenever men desire to make the best use of their resources, their income, their time, or their abilities (all of which have alternative possible uses) the opportunity cost principle is crucially relevant. One has not really learned economics until it has become a habitual part of his thinking and until he has also learned its limitation (that resources may also be used to discover worthy wants as well as to fulfill existing wants) .

Economic systems. Any effort to solve the economic problem by means of increasing production and improving the allocation of resources necessarily involves the development of an economic system (a socioeconomic organization) . For the study of economic systems economists have developed two classificatory schemes. First, there is the classification of the functions of every economy; deciding what to produce, how it shall be produced, how much shall be produced, and for whom the products are produced. The study of economic systems includes a study of how these functions are performed and how they are interrelated. Second, there is the classification of the types of economic systems, ones coordinated by custom, by authority, by elected representatives, and by markets. Most actual economies are mixed; that is, they employ more than one of these types of coordination.

The topics which follow concern mainly our own and similar economics—private enterprise economics. Economics has developed two interrelated systems of ideas for viewing such an economy, a microeconomic picture and a macroeconomic picture.

Microeconomic system of flows, exchanges, markets, and prices. This system involves an understanding of the circular-flow picture of our economy including the flow of goods, services, and productive services and the reverse flow of dollars, all coordinated by means of markets for goods and services and productive services. This view leads ultimately to the concept of general equilibrium and to an understanding of the working of the economic principle in a framework of competitive markets and prices.

Macroeconomic system of flows. This involves an understanding of concepts related to gross national product, national income, aggregate demand, and the relation of consumption, savings, investment, government receipts and expenditures, and international trade to these concepts.

The political-economic problem of citizens. The key political-economic question by means of which the vote of the citizen in a democracy is solicited concerns the nature of the good economic organization: Do we want to elect public officials who will move our economy in the direction of greater reliance on competitive markets or do we want to expand the role of central government by providing through it more of the goods and services we as a people desire? Economics as a social science cannot provide an objectively right answer to this question. It can and should assist one in recognizing the more responsible and competent advocates of one position or the other. The political-economic problem of citizens is ultimately answered by one's value judgments.

Economic problems. The political-economic problem of citizens is most often faced not in terms of any grand choice between "free enterprise or socialism" but in terms of concrete economic problems. Students must learn how to study problems. Indeed the Task Force Report says, "Above all else, economic education should emphasize that rational, objective analysis is needed on economic issues, large and small." [9] The problems approach, according to this report, includes four steps: (1) defining the problem, (2) identifying and ranking the goals, (3) discovering the alternative

[9] *Economic Education and the Schools* (New York: Committee on Economic Development, 1961).

policies, and (4) determining the probable consequences of each alternative. Economics provides an excellent area in which a student can establish a habit of systematic approach to problems (or learns to recognize a competent authority on the problem). Economics, probably better than any other social science, provides a subject-matter in which to discover the pervasiveness of self-interest. When one learns that even he rationalizes his economic self-interest in terms of the public good, an objective approach to economic problems may become possible.

Social goals or values. Thought about the good economy or the good solution to economic problems leads one necessarily to a consideration of social goals or values. Certainly in economics one must learn the meaning and measures of goals closely related to the subject. We want a productive (or efficient) economy. We want a growing economy. We want economic stability (including both a high level of employment and a stable general price level).[10] We want economic security. We want an equitable sharing of the products and opportunities in our economy. We want freedom of choice for producers and consumers, for suppliers of productive services, and for buyers of productive services. These aims must be understood. Whenever they conflict (and often one is to be secured only at the cost of others), the student must learn to choose.

The structure of economics is summarized in the Chart 1. The whole of economics centers in (1) the economic problem, the fact that we must economize in the use of resources for producing goods and services to satisfy in so far as possible our seemingly unlimited wants. From the economic problem emerge two different though related clusters of

[10] *Ibid.,* pp. 43–44.

Chart 1. The structure of economics

(1)
The economic problem
Scarcity
Wants   Resources

S Y S T E M S

(2) *Production and determinants*		(3) *Allocation of resources*
	(4) *Economic systems*	
Factors of production		The econ. prin.
Quan. & qual.		Opportunity cost prin.
Div. of labor	Functions	
Transportation	Types of coord.	Marginal analysis
Communication		
Capital stock		
Technology		
etc.	Private enterprise	
	Economy	

(5)
Microeconomic view
Markets
Product
Productive services
Prices
Exchange
etc.

(6)
Macroeconomic view
GNP, NI
C, I, G, S, T, etc.*

(7) *Political-economic problem of citizens*		(8) *Economic problems*
	P R O B L E M S	
		Probs. approach

(9)
Goals or values
Productivity
Growth
Stability
Equity
Economic security
Economic freedom

* Gross national product, national income, consumption, investment, government, savings, taxes.

concepts, institutions, classifications, and theoretical schemes.

The first cluster concerns how man organizes to make the best use of scarce resources. It includes ideas around (2) production and its determinants, (3) principles to guide the allocation of resources (the economic principle and the opportunity cost principle), and (4) alternative economic systems. For viewing an economic system such as our own (that is, a private enterprise economy), two analytical schemes are of particular use— (5) the microeconomic view and (6) the macroeconomic view.

The second cluster of concepts centers in problems. It originates in the economic problem and includes (7) the problem of societies of men determining what kind of economy they will have. It includes also (8) the many individual economic problems. Common to both are (9) the goals or values by which solutions to problems are to be judged.

This is the structure of economics, including closely related considerations (values) which are essential if economics is to be learned in a framework useful to the generally educated.

As indicated in the opening sentences of this chapter, far more curriculum work has been done by leading scholars in this field than in the other disciplines included in this book. Furthermore, it might be argued that economics lends itself to this type of analysis more readily than the others. As M. L. Frankel says, "Of all the social sciences, economics has perhaps made the greatest gains in developing a formalized structure which, if understood, will help man to bring more order into his life." [11] As would be expected, there are a number of other references which attempt to state a structure of this field. There seems to be little point in including

[11] *Economic Education* (New York: Center for Applied Research in Education, 1965), p. 55.

a variety of these attempts here. This has been done elsewhere. I would, however, like to demonstrate that the statement which has probably attracted the most attention coin-
cides with Leamer's views. I would hypothesize that there is
greater agreement among economists over what should be
taught than in any other area included in this book.

As we have seen, the Committee on Economic Development published the work of a distinguished "task force" in a
pamphlet called *Economic Education and the Schools.*
Forty-two economic concepts and institutions were identified and discussed: (1) scarcity—the need for economizing;
(2) costs—opportunity (or alternative) costs, money costs;
(3) productive resources—factors of production; (4) division of labor, specialization and exchange; (5) economic
production—conversion of resources into desired outputs;
(6) saving, investment, capital formation; (7) labor
productivity; (8) principle of diminishing returns; (9)
demand, supply, price; (10) market; (11) competi-
tion; (12) profit, profit incentive; (13) interdependence—
the price and the market system; (14) economic efficiency;
(15) monopoly, antitrust laws; (16) public utility; (17)
corporation, balance sheet, profit and loss statement; (18)
government expenditures and taxes in allocating resources;
(19) taxes—corporate income tax, personal income tax,
property tax, sales tax, payroll tax; (20) international specialization; (21) tariffs; (22) gross national product, national income, per capita product and income; (23) money
and real income; (24) price level; (25) equation of exchange; (26) aggregate demand (total spending) and components of aggregate demand (consumer spending, business
spending on investment, government spending) ; (27) business cycle, depression, inflation; (28) money, bank deposits
and money creation through bank lending; (29) central

bank—Federal Reserve System; (30) government budget, fiscal policy, public debt; (31) economic growth; (32) underdeveloped areas; (33) the population problem; (34) income as payment for productive services; (35) personal distribution of income; (36) real and money wages; (37) labor unions—collective bargaining; (38) strikes, picketing, closed shop, featherbedding; (39) economic security as a goal; (40) social security, unemployment insurance, old age insurance, private security measures; (41) "farm problem"; and (42) communism as an economic system.

This listing leads us to our final concern in this chapter: What are the problems of teaching economics?

Problems of Teaching Economics

Even though there is more agreement on what should be taught, we are not out of the woods in terms of very real problems for teaching this field. Teaching economics has some headaches, some that are unique to the field and others that are shared with other subjects. Much of the discussion following Leamer's presentation centered on these problems.

1. The inadequacy of the preparation of teachers of economics at the secondary and elementary level is a fact. This point has been made so many times and in so many places that it needs no documentation here. Nevertheless, the problem continues to be serious.[12] Social studies teachers by and large have had little, if any, formal training in economics. Obviously, this deficiency presents a major obstacle to sound teaching.

2. Then there are the stereotypes about the field. Eco-

[12] George Dawson, *Nation-wide Survey on the Education of Teacher-Trainees* (New York: Joint Council on Economic Education, 1967).

nomics is supposed to be dull, difficult, and dogmatic. It is anathema for girls particularly. It is considered to be the least lively of the social sciences. None of these attitudes is justified, but they exist and are widespread.

3. The field does have a large technical vocabulary. The "gobbledygook" not only includes a number of terms that are unique to the field and must be learned, but it uses a lot of words in a technical sense that have quite different everyday meanings. "Good," "investment," "capital," and "rent" are common examples. Learning these terms can lead to dull vocabulary drills.

4. Economics if it is properly taught rushes full speed ahead into controversy. Every significant economic problem has at least two sides on which people take strong stands. Men are not very relaxed about questions that impinge on what they firmly believe is their economic wellbeing. This situation gives rise to fun and excitement in the classroom, but it also places economics teachers in the limelight. The desires of just about every vested interest group are a part of the course of study of economics. The teacher needs to be on the lookout continually for bias in the materials he uses. He must check himself continually to see how his prejudices are influencing what he is teaching and how he is teaching. The degree and heat of the conflict in this area creates problems; the good teacher needs to be aware of the pitfalls, but not back away from controversy.

5. It is very easy for the teaching of economics to become something else. I have already indicated that economics is neither a branch of theology in which the answers to basic value questions are found nor is it a handbook of how-to-do-it information. Teachers can easily fall into either of these traps. Perhaps the most common fault along these lines in secondary schools is to teach a course in how to read labels

and call this economics. Consumer economics is probably valuable, but it is not economics.

6. There is still a shortage of good teaching materials on economic topics for elementary and secondary schools. However, the Joint Council on Economic Education, its state and local affiliates, the curriculum projects identified in Chapter 1, a large number of groups such as the Committee for Economic Development, and commercial publishers have given us enormous help on this matter. But it will always be a problem to some extent, partly because of the final issue, which we should mention now.

7. Change characterizes this field. Scholarship in the field is increasing at a rapid rate. Data in the field are changing at an even more rapid rate. This change creates teaching problems. How does a secondary school teacher keep abreast of the scholarship? How does he know that the data he presents are accurate and objective? Perhaps this problem is the same for all fields, but it seems more acute for economics.

Still, in spite of these problems, economics seem far closer to "the answers" in terms of curriculum than any other field in the social sciences. In fact, economics is close to achieving the exalted state of science and mathematics. Much could be learned from their model.

Suggestions for Further Reading

In addition to the items cited in the notes, the reader may wish to consult these references:

Calderwood, James D. *Economic Ideas and Concepts*. New York: Joint Council on Economic Education, 1964.

Economic Literacy for Americans: A Program for Schools and for Citizens. New York: Committee for Economic Development, 1962.

Key Understandings in Economics. Washington, D.C.: Council for the Advancement of Secondary Education, 1956.

Senesh, Lawrence. *Our Working World.* Chicago: Science Research Associates, 1965. A textbook series for elementary schools. The materials seem to be deterministic.

Suggestions for Grade Placement and Development of Economic Ideas and Concepts. New York: Joint Council on Economic Education, 1964.

Wolf, Ronald H. "Economics," in *The Social Sciences Foundation of the Social Studies.* Ed. John U. Michaelis and A. Montgomery Johnson. Boston: Allyn and Bacon, 1965.

[8]

Government

Professor Alan Altshuler, an extremely able and stimulating young teacher, was our consultant from the field of government. His undergraduate degree is from Cornell and he has two advanced degrees from the University of Chicago, an interesting background for our purposes, since the two schools organize the study of government in quite different ways. He has taught at Swarthmore, at Cornell, and at Makerere College in Uganda and is now at M.I.T., likewise adding to the breadth of his perspective. He is the author, among other works, of an analysis of the city planning process.[1]

As would be expected, no two of our consultants tackled the problem of structure in quite the same way. Altshuler skimmed over the nature, scope, and methods of the field in order to devote himself more fully to a consideration of the topics that he believes should be taught. He did, however, recommend several books that he thought would be helpful on the methodological questions. Let us turn briefly to these matters before we consider Altshuler's ideas regarding the conceptual structure of the field.

1. *The City Planning Process: A Political Analysis* (Ithaca, N.Y.: Cornell University Press, 1965).

Structure and the Social Studies

Definition and Purpose

Not only is it difficult to define the field of government in a way which will be satisfactory to a majority of the scholars in the area; even naming it causes trouble. The most common name is "political science," while some departments use the term "politics." Some scholars in the field strenuously object to the term "political science" on the grounds that all or parts of the field simply do not meet the tests of a science. These critics are using the natural science model. I have used the term "government" mainly because Altshuler used it. I do not know whether or not he attaches any particular significance to the title; he may well have used it only because the department at Cornell has that name. Rather than become involved to any extent in this argument, let us try to define the field and leave the question of the most appropriate title to one side. In this chapter all three titles are used interchangeably.

In the simplest possible terms, the study of government is, as Leslie Lipson says, a "systematic study of the goals, institutions and processes of the state." [2] Now of course, in spite of the conciseness of this statement, one immediately perceives the complexity and the range of interests. This definition leads to a consideration of subject matter traditionally viewed as a part of philosophy, law, history, economics, psychology, sociology, and social psychology in a very direct way, and many other disciplines are associated in a less direct fashion. Polsby, Dentler, and Smith go so far as to claim that political science is not a single discipline, but a "melange of fields." [3] They describe five kinds of political

[2] *The Great Issues of Politics: An Introduction to Political Science* (Englewood Cliffs, N.J.: Prentice-Hall, 1954) , p. 75.

[3] Nelson W. Polsby, Robert A. Dentler, and Paul A. Smith, eds., *Politics and Social Life: An Introduction to Political Behavior* (Boston: Houghton Mifflin, 1963) .

scientists. There are the "political theologians," who are primarily interested in the question of how men ought to live together and govern themselves. There are the "political historians," who want to know how and why people of earlier times have "solved" the problems of establishing necessary controls on the affairs of men. The third group is called the "political engineers." They are interested in reforming the political status quo. They are the actionists and political missionaries. They want to establish new or revised political patterns. They generally assume that the value questions are already solved or should be solved by now. Then there are the "political anecdotalists." They are considered to be the record-keepers. That is, they observe and record what is happening, what actually exists. Their work is mostly descriptive. These are the journalists of the field. Of late they have become very interested in case studies, depth treatments of particular systems, institutions, or issues. Usually, they admit to the lack of generality in their work. Finally, there are the "political behaviorists." Polsby and his co-editors tell us that these are the empirical social scientists in the field. They are interested in observing human behavior, analyzing it, classifying it, uncovering any significant relationships among various parts of it and between it and other factors in the environment; they are seeking generalizations regarding it. There is no doubt that these three authors regard political behaviorism to be the most significant and productive of the political "sciences." Others in the field, naturally, do not feel this way; they say that the behaviorists have gone too far with their attempts at precision, that you cannot study man this way and it would not be desirable if you could.

Professional meetings of political scientists nearly always include a discussion of the nature of the field and what it ought to be doing. The philosophers, social scientists, historians, lawyers, journalists, and social engineers—all of whom call themselves political scientists—get very impatient with each other. In my view there is less agreement in this field regarding the basic goals than in any of the other disciplines included in this book. Harold Lasswell says:

In this bellicose setting, intellectual differences of scope and method are transmuted into fighting ideologies and slogans. In this way "philosophy," morality and religion, manage to oppose "science," "pseudo-science" and "administrative triviality"; in reply the "pursuit of verifiable truth" stands over against the "arrogance" of purported "truth by definition" and "private revelation." Even "mathematics" and "statistics" are fighting words, and "behavioral," "metaphysical" and "legalistic" are expressions of opprobrium or encomium.[4]

These differences have led to a spate of self-evaluation essays and papers—much to the disgust of some members of the profession who believe that this activity is interfering with the production of scholarship in the field. On the other hand, a good many political scientists claim that not nearly enough of this self-study has occurred. Parenthetically, an important leader and "needler" in all of this activity is Professor Charles Hyneman, one of the most respected elder statesmen of the field. His book *The Study of Politics: The Present State of American Political Science*[5] is one of the clearest treatments of the methodological questions available.

To understand this urge to clarify the nature of the field,

---

[4] Harold D. Lasswell, *The Future of Political Science* (New York: Atherton, 1963).

[5] Urbana, Ill.: University of Illinois Press, 1959.

we must remember that political science is a young discipline. Although an interest in the study of government is as old as is an interest in the study of man, most writers in the field admit that a distinct discipline of government did not meaningfully exist in this country until the beginning of the twentieth century. In fact, the beginning of the American Political Science Association in 1903 is commonly used as the starting point for the field. Dwight Waldo, among others, claims that the development of the field was both a part of the scientific movement in academic enterprises and also a part of the reform impulse in political affairs.[6] This double-edged motivation is still a part of the field. Political scientists are still asking whether the field is to reform or is to be a "hard-nosed, cold" science.

Hyneman divides the task of political science into four parts.[7] First, it must accurately and fully describe the legal government. This involves a survey of the organizational structure and of the decision-making process. Included are descriptions of governmental controls, voting procedures, parties, nomination and election procedures, and pressure groups. The acts and policies of the government must also be observed and reported. Finally, outlining the conditions of the social environment of the men living under the government being studied is a necessary part of the descriptive phase.

Second, the field must examine ideas. This involves the analysis of one's own ideas and those of others. The ideas should be taken from all sources including the classics and literature. This phase involves reporting, restating, translating, interpreting, applying, classifying, categorizing, and

[6] *Political Science in the United States of America* (Paris: UNESCO, 1956).
[7] *Study of Politics,* p. 25.

analyzing ideas in an effort to develop a grand political theory (or smaller constituent specific political theories) that will explain the political goals and behavior of men.

The third phase, also related to building theory, is what Hyneman calls "construction of a science." This is the process of bringing ideas and descriptions together, that is, combining facts and ideas, then drawing hypotheses, testing them, and hopefully developing a set of tested generalizations that will support or refute the theoretical constructs.

The fourth task of political science, and a thoroughly legitimate one in Hyneman's view, is to develop "normative doctrine and proposals for social action." This aspect of the field also brings empirical data and theories together, but the result is untested and, frequently, untestable. The doctrine or proposal reflects overtly the scholar's opinions, prejudices, dreams, and hopes for mankind. Sometimes the scholar stops short of presenting a proposal for action; he merely states his views based on his analysis of the facts, or he provides his best guess regarding the most appropriate social doctrine.

But Hyneman readily admits that many of his colleagues do not accept his all-inclusive notion. He believes that the following questions suggest the bases of disagreement: (1) Is the scope of the field too broad? (2) If so, is there an area or two in which we should concentrate—power, for example? (3) How scientific should we be, and should all scholars in the field try to be equally scientific? (4) What should the relationship be among the social sciences? Should the political scientist be participating in a search for a unified social science discipline? (5) What is the legitimate role of values in the study of government? (6) Once we know what the role of values should be in the discipline, how should we go about studying them? For example, should political scientists take normative positions? (Hyneman says yes, but many disagree.) (7) What should be done with the political classics? (8) How much attention and energy should be centered on action—helping to solve current problems by running for office, for example, or serving on the staff of elected officials? The scholars in the field cannot agree on the answers to these questions, and we will not attempt to resolve them here.

Future Directions

Most attempts to evaluate the field of government have something to say about the future of the discipline. Usually, after the writer has shown that there are problems and disagreements, he indicates that there do seem to be some common beliefs and some trends for the future. The lists of trends reported by the various writers differ, in some cases dramatically; but most of the authors would accept most of the points that follow. It should also be said by way of further qualifying these remarks that they may not be entirely consistent. That is, a push in one of these directions might well mean a retreat in another one.

1. There is a trend toward quantification, toward empiricism, toward employing statistical procedures, toward the seeking of generalizations and the drawing of modest and tentative conclusions. Descriptive work that stops short of this will not be generally held in high regard.

2. There appears to be a decreasing interest in the formal institutions of government and an increasing interest in human behavior. As Waldo puts it, "There is a greater interest in the political man or even the social and biological man than in the official man." [8]

[8] *Political Science,* p. 19.

3. There seems to be increased interest in intersystem and intrasystems comparative studies, particularly in cross-cultural comparisons. Again, these must not be just descriptions of two systems but, rather, analyses. Generalizations are sought.

4. There is a new interest in the scientific study of the outcomes of political behavior—law and public policy.

5. There is an ever-expanding concern for political theory. Political scientists are in almost complete agreement that their major task is to find a theoretical base which will explain and clarify the most effective possible relationship between man and the political instruments and institutions he has developed.

At the moment, the field of political science will not accept a single focus for the field, but probably political theory comes as close to this as we can get. The trouble comes, of course, when one tries to be more specific about the meaning of political theory and about the essential elements contained in it. At various times particular political scientists have argued that one idea or concept provides or should provide the key to the understanding of political theory. Power, legal governmental institutions, the process of decision-making, the act of political participation, political statuses and roles, the nature and function of the elite, the means of political communication, and the factors which make a political community unique are such ideas. But it seems impossible to get the majority to accept any one of these important concerns of the field as the prime unifying concept.

Organization

One more means of identifying the scope of the field will be employed—the major subdivisions of the field. Two lists of categories will be presented. One was developed by

Dwight Waldo in 1956 [9] and the other represents the program divisions at the 1966 meeting of the American Political Science Association.[10] I think the similarity is striking and represents more agreement than the controversy in the field would lead us to expect.

Waldo, 1956	*A.P.S.A., 1966*
1. Political theory	1. Political theory
2. Public administration	2. Public administration
3. American government other than federal, including federal-nonfederal governmental relationships	3. State and local government
	4. Judicial processes
4. Judicial affairs	5. International relations
5. International relations and law	6. Political processes
	7. Political modernization in the U.S.
6. Politics, parties, pressure groups	8. Civil order and violence
	9. American government
7. Public opinion, voting and elections	10. Political psychology
	11. Comparative politics—developing systems
8. Public policy	12. Comparative politics—developed systems
9. Executive affairs	13. Comparative politics—communist systems
10. Legislative affairs	
11. Law and jurisprudence	
12. Foreign and comparative government	

A.P.S.A., 1966 note: This list also included several methodological topics which are subsumed under the various categories in the 1956 list.

Methods

In terms of method, political science is not unique. It is a borrower. It uses the techniques that have already been

[9] *Ibid.*, pp. 39–41.

[10] Mimeographed report (1966) of the Executive Director of the American Political Science Association, 1726 Massachusetts Avenue, N.W., Washington, D.C. 20036.

identified in this volume. It is probably true that there is less historical and philosophical research and more empirical work in the field than was formerly true, but humanistic studies still play an important role. As we have seen, the political scientist is determined to find sound political theory. In this search he would be foolish indeed to limit himself to empirical studies of the present. He does many kinds of research and consequently uses many approaches and techniques. His tools do not set his field apart from other disciplines. If government is a discipline, it is because of its subject matter and not because of its methodology.

Francis J. Sorauf has provided a very interesting chapter on methods of inquiry in *Political Science: An Informal Overview*.[11] He tells us that the political scientist works in libraries to analyze documents, voting records, speeches, memoirs, newspapers, debate records, committee reports, census data, letters and memoranda, research reports and monographs, lay and professional periodicals, classic statements and literature, library references and indexes. He interviews, observes, and becomes a participant observer in the field. He uses questionnaires. He sets up controlled experiments on occasion and he engages in simulations. He looks for similarities and differences and relationships. He tries to develop principles and generalizations. He tries to correlate and scale and, therefore, engages in variate and multivariate research. He uses logic in his attempts to explain, interpret, and define. He analyzes in terms of function, role, status, and purpose. He traces the development of ideas historically. He develops case studies. In short, he uses the approaches and techniques of most of his professional colleagues who are also interested in the study of man.

[11] Columbus, Ohio: Merrill, 1965.

Pedagogical Assumptions

Altshuler quite properly began his presentation with some pedagogical assumptions because he thought that they formed an essential base for understanding his conceptual structure.

First, Altshuler is convinced that we "sell kids short," that is, that they are capable of abstract thinking at a higher level than is generally assumed by curriculum-makers. He believes (like Bruner) that high school students, nearly all of them, can profitably grapple with issues and theories important enough to interest scholars in the field. He argues that the test for whether something should be in the curriculum or not ought to be whether the content is fundamentally true, important, and interesting from the viewpoint of a mature scholar in the field. Content should not be selected for its simplicity or on the availability of watered-down teaching materials.

Second, there are two central reasons for teaching government (and probably any subject) according to Altshuler: to arouse intellectual curiosity in the ideas and techniques of the discipline, and to teach students to think critically and analytically about issues in this area of knowledge. These objectives are important in understanding the curriculum which follows. The reader is invited to analyze Altshuler's structure in terms of his statement of purpose.

The third assumption is that while the range of topics of interest for the mature scholar in the field of government is vast, and while there is a host of interesting, true, and significant things to know, the teacher would be well-advised to teach a few topics well rather than to expose children to a welter of facts and concepts. Further, it is crucial even on the few topics that are selected that children understand that what they are learning is only partial and tentative truth. Altshuler is distressed by the number of college freshman who think they know far more than they actually do.

Fourth, ideas about government should and must be taught in history and other classes, but most children should not take a separate course in government per se before their senior year in high school. Despite the exceptions, most children before this time do not possess the general intellectual maturity and the necessary background information.

Fifth, while as we shall see there are some concepts from government that Altshuler thinks ought to be taught to all, he believes the context and teaching approach should vary. He outlined three curricula, one for college-bound pupils in situations in which the teacher has complete freedom to select the context for teaching the concepts he wishes to teach, one for teachers who must abide by the decision of the state or some other authority to teach a course in American government, and one for children who were not likely to go on to college. Obviously Altshuler does not favor the American government requirement.

His sixth and final assumption is "that the way to arouse student interest in government is to focus on rather stark choices and dangers, that is to say, on highly dramatic issues and contrasts." [12] He is interested then in a problems or issues approach where sharp conflict and contradictions exist. At this point he again emphasized that the contexts or particular topics ought to change. The ability of the pupils as we have seen is one determining variable, but the teacher should also consider what items are of particular interest to the children.

The reader will note that throughout Altshuler's recommendations, ideas about teaching the subject are offered.

[12] Speech at Cornell University, April 1965.

One simply could not help but get the impression that he truly enjoys teaching, a view too often missing among research-oriented scholars.

Curriculum I

Altshuler believes that the curriculum for college-bound students ought to be largely in the hands of individual teachers, but he gave some suggestions: "The fundamental idea which ought to be at the heart of all curricula in government is that politics provides the framework of order for civilization. It is reasonable to claim that the political system is determined by social, cultural, and economic patterns, but the reverse is also true. At any time the political system, and political mores, and political events can make the whole difference between kinds of personal lives that men can lead and the kinds of persons that civilizations can produce." [13] The core then of political study is to appreciate the impact of politics and government on the lives of men. To repeat, this idea is basic to all three curricula.

Altshuler begins Curriculum I with the idea that stable democracies—governments in which the ideals of decency, truth, and personal liberty are continually and relatively successfully sought—are extremely rare in history. In considering why this is so, the student should trace the development of the democratic idea. He must understand that throughout history many thinkers have argued that democracy will not work in large states. He must read and study carefully the relevant passages of the Federalist Papers in which the idea of representative democracy as a better form than direct democracy is promoted in a systematic way for the first time.

This idea should be further developed by a careful con-

[13] *Ibid.*

sideration of whether or not representative democracy will work in the so-called developing national states of the contemporary world. Altshuler suggests that the students read Seymour Lipset's brillant analysis of the requisites of democracy found in *Political Man*.[14] A study of the notion that few of the developing nations are ready for democracy and that few will make it in the foreseeable future would be highly useful. Students should begin to get an awareness of the impact in history of social revolutions.

As an outgrowth of the above, the student should be "stretched" to read and think at as high a level as possible about the philosophical issues associated with political democracy. He should grapple with the question of the extent to which modern democratic theories depend on specific assumptions about the nature of man and on particular educational and moral theories. He should think about the nature of "good citizenship" and political morality. He should consider the ideas of Thucydides or Plato for the classical view, and the debate between Hobbes and Locke as well as the Federalist Papers should be introduced for a more modern interpretation. Pupils who have the necessary ability should read parts of these works, and the rest should be exposed to some of the ideas in them by the teacher. Altshuler believes the best way to pull these ideas together is to study a democracy that has failed. He discussed the failure of the Weimar Republic, but apparently there are other equally valid choices.

The impact of totalitarianism on the lives of ordinary individuals should be studied. Again he would employ the case-study approach. If the Weimar Republic has been used earlier, the Nazi period would offer the advantage of continuity. But regardless of the state selected, government by

[14] Garden City, N.Y.: Doubleday, 1960.

terror, mass propaganda, and the attitudes of insiders and outsiders during the regime should be studied. The central question might be, How did it happen?

Students should study war and the "changing culture of warfare." Ideas such as the difficulty of arriving at norms for behavior in wartime, and the difficulty of diplomacy without international morality are important. The attempts throughout history, even though usually "insincere," to abolish war should be studied. The savagery and brutality of war should not be disguised. Students should seriously and systematically consider the various theories for the causes for war. For example, the Marxian position and the mental illness idea might be introduced and criticized. Altshuler suggests *Man, the State, and War* by Kenneth Waltz [15] as a good place to begin this study.

Another important concept and one that Altshuler would also treat historically is nationalism. What are the bases of nationhood? Why are tribal rather than national loyalties so strong in some of the newer states, and why are provincial and state loyalties so significant in some of the older nations? This subject would also provide an opportunity to return to some of the earlier philosophical questions raised, this time taking the form of what claim national states can and should justifiably make on individuals. A large number of case studies are available for illustrating the contemporary importance of national and subnational loyalties, but, to repeat, these depth studies should follow a historical survey.

This topic would naturally flow, according to our consultant, into a consideration of personal liberty in history. The interacting development of the ideas of natural law and natural rights should be explored. The significance of

[15] New York: Columbia University Press, 1959.

freedom of expression would provide Altshuler's context for teaching personal liberty. That is, he would study freedom of expression in depth as a means of understanding personal liberty.

Finally, this first curriculum, the one which Altshuler obviously thought was most desirable, would include the exploration of some of the contemporary theories and the resultant problems of representation. A cluster of questions would be studied: Is the central idea of representative government to govern or to represent? How do these notions conflict? What are advantages and disadvantages of a nationally disciplined party system? For example, our consultant would have students study Walter Lippmann's thesis of the incompatibility of our form of democracy with a sound foreign policy.[16] What election and nomination processes are available to us? What are the strengths and weaknesses of various schemes?

In all of these instances, Altshuler would use historic and comparative contrasts. In most he would use a case study. Some would be American, but the nationality of the case should depend on the knowledge of the teacher and the situation in which he finds himself. In all situations children would read a great deal, but "never in a textbook."

Curriculum II

The second curriculum outlined was also for bright high school seniors, but this time for classrooms required to study American government. (It seems to me that Curriculum I is also a study of American government, but Altshuler sees it as comparative government.) Again, the content would be arranged into a "great political issues" course using a historical approach. The first concept is equality. Altshuler is

16 *The Public Philosophy* (New York: Little, Brown, 1955).

interested in having the pupils study various meanings this term has had in American history. The focus would be on the extent to which equality has been the fundamental ideal of American politics. He would expose students to Gunnar Myrdal's ideas about the core of the American reality and the American creed.[17] He recommends that they read Michael Young's *Rise of Meritocracy*.[18] After the philosophical problems of definition and the changes in meaning have been briefly explored, Altshuler suggests a depth case study of the American Negro and his role in politics: "No other phase of American politics has so consistently threatened our system." Almost every contemporary political question of importance is connected with the racial issue—reapportionment, housing, welfarism, urbanism, separation of church and state, to name only a few. The class should explore the American perception of equality within the context of the Negro's role in the political system. Closely related is the concept of justice. Equality and justice should be examined concurrently.

The second major concept is democracy, and Altshuler raises the same question: To what extent is democracy the central ideal of American politics? The theme of this unit is the development in our history from little faith in democracy as evidenced by the views of the founding fathers to an increasing belief in the right of common men to control their destinies. The teacher might begin by asking his students to uncover all the ways that the writers of the Constitution demonstrated their lack of faith in democracy, and then see how many of these checks on democracy have been eliminated. The student should then be led to try to uncover the relationships among equality, justice, and

[17] *American Dilemma* (New York: Harper, 1944).
[18] Baltimore: Penguin, 1963.

democracy—to see the points at which they have come into conflict.

The third concept is liberty. How do justice, democracy, liberty, and equality relate to one another? How are they distinct and yet a part of the same fabric? The theme here would be the "bigness" of government or the changing role of government. How big is too big; how small is too small?

The fourth theme, not really a concept, is the problem of foreign policy-making in modern times. Again, Lippman's claim that sound foreign policy is incompatible with our system as it now exists is the issue. The class should examine some of the puzzles of post-World War II foreign policy-making. How does a large standing army affect both our contemporary foreign policy and our traditions? How does the development and strengthening of clandestine institutions, particularly the C.I.A., affect our relations with other nations and our processes for determining foreign policy? How does contemporary news management affect our traditional ways of looking at international affairs? Is there any significance in the old idea that sea powers can be effective democracies but land powers cannot? How are we to deal with the fact of the complexity of our life, a complexity which makes it impossible for Congressmen, let alone voters, to be "intelligent on international questions?"

Altshuler would then have the student study the changing concept of freedom of expression in our society. What have we said and what have we actually done in this regard? Topics from the early sedition laws to long haircuts in high schools can be involved. The teacher's problem will be to decide which examples to select. An almost essential subidea is civil disobedience. Students should have a reasoned position on this matter.

No American government class is complete without a

study of the Marxist view of man and of capitalism. Altshuler's approach to this topic would be the shock technique. He would lead the class to see how many Americans accept much of the Marxian view. A crucial item associated with this is the relative absence in our political system until recently of economic class politics.

This consideration should lead into a study "of the nature of the American party system—the obstacles of achieving party unity in the United States, the relationship of the party system to the minority veto system of American politics, and the paradox that the founders were hostile to parties but created a constitutional system that almost surely could not have worked without parties as the glue to hold the separated powers together." [19] How can and does an undisciplined party system work?

Finally the group should study the local governmental system in terms of each of the other seven themes. How does our local governmental system support and refute our values of equality, liberty, justice, and democracy?

Curriculum III

As was said in the introduction to this material on the conceptual structure of government, Professor Altshuler believes that it is necessary to have at least three curricula. The last one is for students who are not likely to go on to college. I believe that the three are really quite similar, that only specific contexts have changed. I think the overlap is apparent, but to do justice to his idea, I will present briefly an outline of the third curriculum.

The first idea is to have students see how one manages to get the American political system to work for him. Locally, how one obtains better schools and better garbage collec-

[19] Altshuler's Cornell speech, April 1965.

tion. Nationally, how one gets a government which promotes the economic well-being of its citizens and at the same time protects their individuality. The children should study an organized pressure campaign on some topic of local interest, any topic will do. How did the pressure group get started? Who were its leaders? What techniques did it use? How was it effective and ineffective?

This discussion would lead to a study of the political party system in this country. Most of the questions identified in Curriculum II would be examined. Special attention would be given to the problems of organizing lower socioeconomic groups into parties or into any other effective pressure group. The fact that the subgroups of lower socioeconomic classes spend much of their energy fighting each other should be explored. Again the case study approach is recommended. This time the class would center on the study of how an important piece of social legislation is passed; Altshuler recommends the Civil Rights Law of 1964.

Then the students should be led to a consideration of democracy, liberty, justice, and equality as ideals of our system. Altshuler said that he would "indoctrinate more and shock less" with this group than he would with brighter pupils. In the discussion which followed his presentation, however, he seemed to back away from this view. When one of the teachers in the group took the position that these children need to be taught to question and think even more than bright kids and that they could do it, Altshuler seemed relieved. He seemed fearful of giving less able students the freedom to question American ideals because he doubted their interest in so doing, but he emphasized that he has never taught pupils of this sort. At any rate, Altshuler would dramatize and emphasize freedom of expression and tolerance with these classes. He believes that working-class "anti-civil libertarianism" must be attacked.

Finally, Altshuler would have these classes study a few of the important political problems of our times. No one of them is essential, and the teacher should be free to select the one or more that he thinks most appropriate. Altshuler tentatively suggested foreign policy, the conflict between economic growth for the society and economic loss for an individual as in the case of technological unemployment, the proper political role of unions, and the "dangers of too much democracy."

Summary

Professor Altshuler aptly summarized his position: "I tried at the beginning of this presentation," he said, "to indicate my approach to introductory teaching, and thus the criteria that I would apply in setting forth the content of my curricula. I have presented my curricula as illustrative, however, and thus you may still ask whether I believe that there is a body of essential content which should be taught to all students in the twelfth grade. My answer, implicit in the curricula that I have outlined, is that I do not consider any factual material indispensable. I do think that American students should, however, grapple to some extent with the history of, and the controversies surrounding, several great objectives of our national life. I think that some of these ideals can be best dramatized without being bound to an American curriculum, but the ideas themselves should be at the core of any curriculum. Probably the most important of them are democracy, equality, liberty, and justice. Closely related to them today are of course the ideas of nationalism, warfare, and national security—the American view of political parties, totalitarianism, free expression, civil rights, representation, and some classic notions of political philosophy. These verbal symbols cover many shades of meaning, and they require concrete illustrations for dramatization. They are the core stuff of politics, however, and they make clear the way in which politics is indeed the maintenance of an ordered framework for civilization. I consider it far more important to dramatize these issues than to teach, say, the main outlines of the American political system in abstract." [20]

Suggestions for Further Reading

In addition to the items cited in the notes, the reader may wish to consult these references:

Easton, David. *The Political System: An Inquiry into the State of Political Science.* New York: Knopf, 1963.

Goals for Political Science. (Report of the Committee for the Advancement of Teaching, American Political Science Association.) New York: William Sloan Associates, Inc., 1959.

Van Dyke, Vernon. *Political Science: A Philosophical Analysis.* Stanford, Cal.: Stanford University Press, 1960.

Young, Roland, ed. *Approaches to the Study of Politics.* Evanston, Ill.: Northwestern University Press, 1958.

For sources of substantive works on various topics in government I recommend the annotated bibliography:

Connery, Robert H., Richard H. Leach, and Joseph Zikmund, *Reading Guide In Politics and Government.* Washington, D.C.: National Council for the Social Studies, N.E.A., 1966.

Two other recent N.C.S.S. publications which are useful are:

Riddle, Donald H., and Robert S. Cleary, eds. *Political Science in the Social Studies.* Washington, D.C.: National Education Association, 1966.

Robinson, Donald W. *Promising Practices in Civic Education.* Washington, D.C.: National Education Association, 1967.

[20] *Ibid.*

[9]

Concluding Remarks

The current palaver over the issue of social studies revision cannot help but lead to a more balanced and informed approach to the curriculum revision problem and to the teaching of social studies in the elementary and secondary schools. By adding our voices to the discussion, we hope to have contributed some insight into the relevance of the theory of structure to the practice of teaching and learning in particular disciplines and in the social studies as a whole.

To be sure, our consultants could speak only for certain fields—government or political science, geography, economics, sociology, anthropology, and history. Other fields could have been included—social psychology, for example. But we believe that the ones that are represented are the most likely to have an impact on the social studies curriculum of the future.

Our goal in this volume has been to share with the reader our frustrating but fascinating search for a clearer understanding of the idea that is shaping most of the developments in social studies—structure. He has no doubt noticed that we have raised more questions than we have answered. We have not uncovered a unifying curriculum theory that solves the persistent questions of what to teach, when, how, and why. Indeed, some of the consultants and a few of our study group have rejected the notion of structure outright; certainly a majority of us have rejected it as it relates to history. Most of us do believe, however, that structure provides the best foundation yet uncovered for many areas of the curriculum.

Index

Index